Real English in American Culture

BIG POT

BIG POT ①

Author Jack McBain
Publisher Chung Kyudo
Editors Kwon Minjeong, Cho Sangik
Designers Jeong Hyunseok, Lee Seunghyun
Photo Credit www.shutterstock.com

First Published in September 2020
By Darakwon, Inc.
Darakwon Bldg., 211, Munbal-ro, Paju-si, Gyeonggi-do 10881
Republic of Korea
Tel: 82-2-736-2031 (Ext. 550)

ISBN 978-89-277-0982-4 14740
     978-89-277-0981-7 14740 (set)

www.darakwon.co.kr

Main Book / Free MP3 Available Online
9 8 7 6 5 4 3   24 25 26 27 28

Real English in American Culture

BIG POT

Jack McBain

DARAKWON

Contents

To the Students

BIG POT is a two-level series for adult and young adult English language learners. This dynamic series contains material appropriate for students ranging from a beginner level to an intermediate level. It is designed to provide students with basic background knowledge about American culture and to help them learn English expressions related to it. Each book in the series provides interesting, thought-provoking material in order to meet the linguistic needs of a diverse community of language learners.

BIG POT 1 has twelve units, each of which consists of a warm-up, three supporting lessons, a wrap-up, and a reading. The book covers numerous aspects of American culture through stimulating conversations. Each conversation provides the context for supplementary grammar, language point, and speaking activities. Students will find topics such as small talk, restaurants & tipping, and entertainment interesting and relevant to living, studying, and working abroad. By practicing conversations related to life in the United States, students will gain a better understanding of the cultural nuances which exist in the large cultural landscape which is America.

As a multi-skill course book, *BIG POT* introduces essential linguistic and cultural information to students. Students will have the opportunity to read about American culture, practice contextually accurate dialogues with one another, answer interesting grammar and language point questions, and finally, participate in a variety of interesting speaking activities with partners and small groups. The purpose of this book is to provide context to the language, a context which will give students access and insight into how Americans actually use the language in everyday life.

Jack McBain

Author's Acknowledgments

The author would like to express his utmost gratitude to the editor Minjeong Kwon. Without her tireless work and guidance, this project would not have been possible. He would also like to acknowledge the contributions of Darakwon management and the graphic design team. Finally, he would like to extend a heartfelt thanks to his family, who has been incredibly patient during the writing process.

Structure of the Book

Discuss the Following Questions
Students will be given some general discussion questions related to the unit's topic.

Introduction to the unit topic
Students will be introduced to the unit's topic with a short reading and some vocabulary related to the unit's topic.

Language Focus
Students will be able to acquire information related to a particular language or grammar point from the dialogue and solve problems related to it.

Conversation
Each unit has three conversations. Students will be able to listen to a dialogue and then practice it with a partner.

Speak Out
Students will be given a speaking activity in which they will be able to work in pairs or small groups.

Wrap It Up
Students will be given a vocabulary writing task and speaking tasks which will summarize the material covered in the unit.

Just So You Know
Students will be given an additional reading passage which will discuss a particular aspect of American culture and the unit's topic.

Plan of the Book

Unit	Title	Topic	Conversation
01	Greetings from America	Greetings & Titles	- Greetings between Friends and Family Members - Greetings at a Job Interview - Greetings between a Professor and a Student
02	Making Small Talk	Small Talk	- Making Small Talk about General Topics - Making Small Talk at Parties - Making Small Talk When in Line
03	Sit-down Restaurants	Restaurants & Tipping	- Ordering at a Sit-down Restaurant - Asking for the Check - Customers with Special Diets
04	A Shopper's Paradise	Shopping	- At a Clothing Store - At a Garage Sale - At a Supermarket
05	Let's Party!	Parties	- At a Dinner Party - At a Christmas Party - At a Cocktail Party
06	Getting Around Town	Transportation	- Taking the Bus - Asking a Bus Driver about a Destination - Ridesharing Apps
07	Entertainment	Entertainment	- Buying Movie Tickets - Buying Concert Tickets - Going to the Park
08	More than Just Great Coffee	Coffee	- Ordering a Cup of Coffee - A First Date at a Coffee Shop - Coming Over for a Cup of Coffee
09	Bars and Nightclubs	Drinking Culture	- Trying to Get into the Bar - At the Bar - Designated Drivers
10	Fast Food	Fast Food	- Ordering at a Fast-food Restaurant - At the Drive-thru - At the Deli
11	Holidays in America	Holidays	- Thanksgiving Dinner - Opening Presents on Christmas Morning - The 4th of July
12	Cooking for Fun	Cooking	- Cooking Pasta Together - Baking Chocolate Chip Cookies - Asking for a Recipe

Language Focus	Reading
- Formal and informal greetings - Titles based on a person's gender and marital status - Titles based on a person's educational status	What Are Some Commonly Used Gestures in America?
- Tag questions - Negative questions - Embedded questions	Proper Small Talk Topics
- Taking an order / Ordering food - Tipping your server - Special diets such as the vegetarian, vegan, pescatarian, or ketogenic diet	When and Where Do I Tip?
- Clothing fits - Making on offer / Rejecting an offer - Prepositions of place	Can I Return This?
- Indirect requests - *must* / *have to* / *'ve got to* - *used to* vs. Present perfect tense	College House Parties
- Indicating frequency - Making sure the bus is heading in the right direction - Giving directions	Too Much Traffic!
- Asking for identification / Common forms of identification - Telling time - Blended words (Reductions)	Different Hobbies in Different Places
- Adding spices and flavoring to foods and beverages - Apologizing and giving reasons - Expressions for containers	Coffee Today vs. Coffee in the Past
- Saying your date of birth - Opening a tab / Keeping the tab open / Closing the tab - The first conditional	Where's Your Perfect Nightclub?
- Making substitutions - Asking for repetition - *a lot of* / *a little* / *a few* / *too much* / *too many*	Do You Usually Supersize It?
- Positive adjectives before nouns - Comparative adjectives - *not as* (adjective) *as ~*	Some Smaller Holidays
- Cooking instructions - Measurements and conversions - Most common food allergies	Eating at Home in America

Greetings from America

🔊 Track **01**

American Greeting Etiquette

When addressing people by name in American English, we often use different titles depending on our relationships with the other people. Children usually refer to their parents as mom and dad. Brothers, sisters, and cousins are usually addressed by only their first names. We also use first names to address our friends, classmates, and coworkers because our relationships with these groups are generally equal. When we address someone by that person's first name only, we are speaking informally with that person.

It is important to remember that in American culture, casual or informal greetings with

acquaintances, not friends or family, should always be positive. If a casual acquaintance asks how you are doing, your reply should be that you are fine even if you are having a terrible day. It would be awkward for you to say you were having a terrible day.

In formal situations, the rules regarding good etiquette change. We use formal addresses when we are speaking with teachers, bosses, professors, and customers. A formal address in American English includes a title and the person's last name. If you are unsure about which form of address to use, use a formal address.

Conversation 1 Greetings between Friends and Family Members

Track 02

A There are a number of common greetings that American English speakers use in their daily lives. Here are several conversations between some friends and family members. Listen and practice the conversations with a partner.

The following conversations are between friends and family members.

Amanda	Good afternoon, Walter!
Walter	Hi, Amanda. It's already 2:00 p.m. Would you like to get some lunch?
Amanda	Sure. I'm starving!
Alan	What's up, Nina?
Nina	Not much, Alan. What's up with you?
Alan	Nothing much. I'm just busy with work.
Robert	Hey there, Sangmi.
Sangmi	Hey, Robert.
Robert	Have you eaten breakfast yet?
Sangmi	No, not yet. Let's go to the cafeteria together.
Daughter	Hey there, Dad! How's it going?
Dad	I'm okay, but I'm a little sore after my gym workout.

⊘ Words to Know   starving   sore   workout

B Practice the conversation with a partner. Use the information in the box below.

A ¹ _____ , (your partner's name). How are things?

B They're ² _____ . How are things with you, (your partner's name)?

A Pretty good. Have you had ³ _____ yet?

B No, not yet.

A Let's get some.

B That sounds ⁴ _____ !

1	2	3	4
Hi	great	breakfast	good
Hello	fine	lunch	wonderful
Hey	wonderful	dinner	great

Language Focus

A When to use formal and informal greetings isn't always clear to English language learners. Below is a chart which provides the subtle differences between some formal and informal greetings.

Formal	Informal (Casual)
Good morning.	Hi.
Good afternoon.	Hey.
Good evening.	Hi there! / Hey there! / Hello there!
Hello.	How's it going?
How are you?	How are things? / How's everything?
How are you doing?	What's up? / What's new?

B Choose and write the correct greetings in the blanks. Then, practice with a partner.

1. A _____ (*Good morning / Good afternoon*), Samantha.

B Morning? It's one o'clock in the afternoon.

A Oh, my gosh! I mean _____ (*good afternoon / good evening*).

I had no idea it was that late. I guess I lost track of time while studying in the library.

2. A _____ (*What's up / Hello*), Professor Jameson.

B _____ (*Hey / How are you doing*), Michael?

A I'm doing great. Thanks.

3. A _____ (*Hey there / Hello*), Dad! How's it going?

B Great! _____ (*Good morning / How's it going*) with you?

A Not bad. I have a lot of English homework though.

Speak Out

Look at the pictures and practice using appropriate greetings based on your relationships with the people.

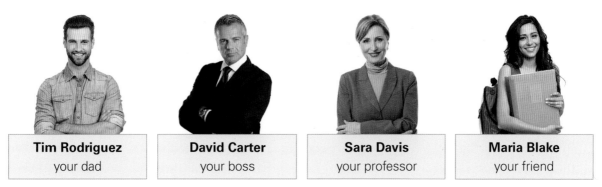

Tim Rodriguez	**David Carter**	**Sara Davis**	**Maria Blake**
your dad	your boss	your professor	your friend

Hey, Dad! How's it going?

Conversation ❷ *Greetings at a Job Interview*

🔊 Track 03

A During job interviews, you should use formal greetings and appropriate titles. This is a conversation between an interviewee and an interviewer. Listen and practice the conversation with a partner.

Sheila Johnston is interviewing for an internship with Eileen Wong.

Sheila Excuse me, ma'am. Do you know where I can find Ms. Eileen Wong?

Eileen May I ask what this is in regard to?

Sheila Of course. I have an interview with her for an internship this morning.

Eileen Oh, you must be Sheila Johnston.

Sheila Yes, that's correct.

Eileen Hi. I'm Eileen Wong. It's nice to meet you, Miss Johnston.

Sheila Hello, Ms. Wong. It's a pleasure to meet you, too.

Eileen Please call me Ellie. Everyone calls me that. You're earlier than I expected.

Sheila I'm really sorry about that. I'm an exchange student, so I'm not familiar with the city yet. I guess I left home a bit too early.

Eileen You're eager. I like that. Follow me to my office. We'll conduct the interview there.

✅ **Words to Know** in regard to familiar eager conduct

B Practice the conversation with a partner. Use the information in the box below.

A Do you know where I can find ¹ 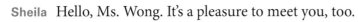 ?

B May I ask what this is in regard to?

A Sure. I have an interview with him/her for an internship at ² 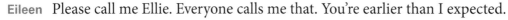 .

B I'm ³ _____ . You must be ⁴ _____ ?

A Yes, that's right. I left my home an hour ago because it's rainy. That's why I'm early.

B That's okay. Let's do the interview now. Come with me to my office.

1	2	3	4
Mr. James Sterling	eight o'clock	James Sterling	Miss Hyemi Kang
Ms. Francine Park	9:30	Francine Park	Mr. Peter Strauss
Mrs. Carrie Dunlop	a quarter to eleven	Carrie Dunlop	Miss Wanda Frankel

Language Focus

A Titles should be used when addressing someone formally in English. In English, we use these titles and the person's last name. Below is a chart that shows which titles should be used based on the person's gender and marital status.

Title	Mr.	Mrs.	Miss	Ms.
Gender and Marital Status	Male / Married, Unmarried, or Unknown	Female / Married	Female / Unmarried	Female / Married, Unmarried, or Unknown

B Write the correct titles in the blanks based on the person's gender and known marital status.

1. (Sarah Williams / married / marital status known by John Erickson)

John Erickson: "Good morning, _____ Williams."

2. (Cindy Wu / unmarried / marital status unknown by Chen Winn)

Chen Winn: "How are you doing, _____ Wu?"

3. (Eileen Wong / married / marital status known by Bert Chrysler)

Bert Chrysler: "Good morning, _____ Wong. I hope you had a nice weekend."

4. (Fred Merriman / unmarried / marital status unknown by Alice Clemens)

Alice Clemens: "Good evening, _____ Merriman. How are things?"

5. (Erica Jung / unmarried / marital status known by Jiho Kim)

Jiho Kim: "Hello, _____ Jung. I have that report you asked for."

Speak Out | Class Activity

Write the full names and marital statuses of four students in your class. Then, practice greeting each person formally by using his or her correct title and last name.

Title	Full Name	Marital Status

Good afternoon, Mrs. Kelly.
How are you, Mr. McDonald?

Conversation ③ *Greetings between a Professor and a Student*

🎧 Track 04

A In America, some professors prefer informal greetings with students while others prefer formal greetings. When unsure, use a formal greeting. If the professor asks you to address him or her informally, you may use an informal greeting from that point on. This is a conversation between a professor and his student. Listen and practice the conversation with a partner.

Sukyung runs into her professor on campus.

Sukyung Good morning, Dr. Merkel.

Professor Morning, Sukyung. Just call me Richard.

Sukyung Okay. Good morning, Richard.

Where are you heading?

Professor I'm on my way to my first class.

Where are you heading?

Sukyung I'm going to the library. I have to work on some homework assignments.

Professor Have you finished your English essay for my class?

Sukyung *(sheepishly)* Not yet, but I'm going to get it done.

Professor Don't forget that it's due on Monday.

Sukyung I won't. I'm going to finish it soon.

Professor Good. Well, I've got to get going. See you in class, Sukyung.

Sukyung Okay. Goodbye, Dr. Mer… oops… Richard!

Professor Hahaha. Goodbye, Sukyung!

⊘ **Words to Know**   run into   assignment   due

B Practice the conversation with a partner. Use the information in the box below.

A ¹ _____ , Dr. Miller.

B Hi, Carrie. ² _____ .

A Okay, ³ _____ . Where are you heading?

B I'm on my way to teach a class. Where are you heading?

A I'm going to the ⁴ _____ . I have to study for a test.

B That sounds great. Well, I've got to get going. See you later!

1	2	3	4
Good morning	Refer to me as Alan	Alan	dormitory (dorm)
Hello	Use my first name, Janine	Janine	student center
Good afternoon	Call me Bernard	Bernard	library

Language Focus

A   There are additional titles that can be used when addressing someone formally. Below is a chart that shows which titles should be used based on the person's educational status.

Title	Dr.	Dr.	Professor
Educational Status	doctor of medicine (M.D.) / professional degree	doctor of philosophy (Ph.D.) / refers to a degree in various fields	an instructor at a university or college

B   Write the correct titles in the blanks.

1. (Jodie Franklin is a doctor of medicine and works in a hospital.)

Jodie Franklin's patient: "Hello, _____ Franklin."

2. (Maria Cordova is a professor at Capital City University and has a Ph.D. in Korean literature.)

Maria Cordova's student: "How are you doing, _____ Cordova?"

3. (Jack Moreland is a professor at Smith College, but he does not have a Ph.D.)

Jack Moreland's student: "Hi, _____ Moreland."

4. (James O'Reilly is a professor at his city's public university. He has a Ph.D. in economics.)

James O'Reilly's student: "Good morning, _____ O'Reilly!"

Speak Out | Pair Work

Act out the role-plays with a partner. Use appropriate titles for formal situations.

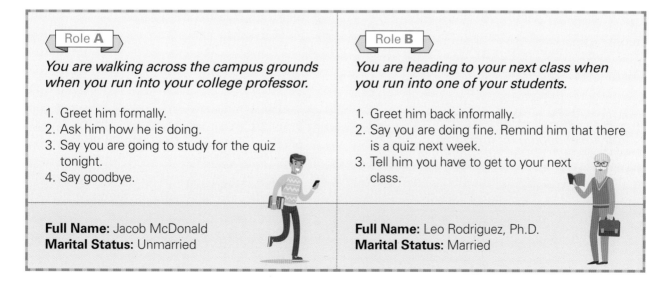

Role **A**	Role **B**
You are walking across the campus grounds when you run into your college professor.	*You are heading to your next class when you run into one of your students.*
1. Greet him formally.	1. Greet him back informally.
2. Ask him how he is doing.	2. Say you are doing fine. Remind him that there is a quiz next week.
3. Say you are going to study for the quiz tonight.	3. Tell him you have to get to your next class.
4. Say goodbye.	
Full Name: Jacob McDonald **Marital Status:** Unmarried	**Full Name:** Leo Rodriguez, Ph.D. **Marital Status:** Married

Wrap It Up

Vocabulary Check **Complete the sentences by using the words in the box.**

| assignment | starving | due | conduct | eager |

1. I'm _____. Let's get some snacks.

2. Thank you for letting me _____ this interview.

3. The student received a poor grade because he did not submit his last _____ .

4. Julian is _____ for the new semester to begin.

5. The report is _____ next week.

Situation Talk **Create profiles for the following people by choosing names and marital statuses for the people in the role-plays. Then, role-play each situation with a partner.**

	Role-Play 1		Role-Play 2
A	Name: Marital Status:	A	Name: Marital Status:
B	Name: Marital Status:	B	Name: Marital Status:

Role-Play 1 (informal)

You are entering the classroom when you see your classmate.

1. Greet him or her.
2. Ask him or her if he or she has had lunch.
3. Invite him or her to lunch after class.

You are sitting in the classroom when you see your friend enter the classroom.

1. Greet him or her back.
2. Say you haven't. Say you are hungry.
3. Accept his or her lunch invitation.

Role-Play 2 (formal)

You are shopping for groceries at the supermarket when you run into your boss.

1. Greet him or her.
2. Ask him or her how he or she is doing.
3. Tell him or her to have a nice time at the party.
4. Say goodbye.

You are at the supermarket when you run into your employee.

1. Greet him or her back.
2. Say you are fine. Tell him or her you are buying wine for a party.
3. Say thank you and that you will see him or her on Monday morning.

What Are Some Commonly Used Gestures in America?

Track 05

Americans use a variety of physical gestures when speaking with others; however, the most common one is the handshake. Americans often shake hands when they first meet someone or when they see an acquaintance they have not seen for a while. To shake hands, you just clasp the other person's hand with your right hand and slightly move it up and down. Americans usually shake hands with the right hand. Do not squeeze so tightly that you hurt the other person's hand, but do not let your hand go limp either. A firm handshake is a sign of confidence in the United States.

With close friends and family members, people in the United States often share an embrace, or a hug, when they see each other. They hug by wrapping their arms around the other person. This is a sign of intimacy between two people, so you must remember that hugging is inappropriate in the workplace. If you are close friends with a coworker, or colleague, hugging outside of the workplace is fine, but a polite hello is more appropriate in the workplace.

Another common gesture is the wave. Americans usually wave when they see another person they know but are too far away to shake hands or hug. Waving and saying hi or hello is very common. In formal situations, such as business meetings, it is much better to avoid waving and to wait until you are close enough to shake hands. Then, you can greet the other person formally.

An informal, but very common gesture, is the high-five. Americans high-five when they see their friends or when something good happens. For example, teammates often high-five one another when one of the players on a soccer team scores a goal. Remember that the high-five is informal and should be used outside of the workplace.

Read the article. Check T for true or F for false.

1. American people don't hug, even though they are close friends.   T ☐ / F ☐
2. Waving is common in the U.S. if friends are too far away to shake hands.   T ☐ / F ☐
3. The high-five is a gesture often used at the beginning of meetings.   T ☐ / F ☐

Unit
02

Making Small Talk

American Small Talk Dos and Don'ts

Americans make small talk in order to avoid uncomfortable silences in social situations involving strangers or those they do not know very well. There are a number of topics that are safe in most situations in America. These topics include the weather, hobbies, current events, sports, and entertainment.

For example, when meeting someone for the first time, you may ask this person what he or she does in his or her free time. This is a completely appropriate question to ask when making small talk with someone. But be careful because even hobbies can be deeply personal to people.

When asking personal questions, even about safe topics, it is best to keep your questions general. You can ask someone you have just met at a party what he or she does for a living, but it would be totally inappropriate to ask that person how much money he or she earns. That kind of information would be considered too personal to discuss with a stranger or an acquaintance.

Discuss the following questions.

1. What is small talk? Is making small talk common in your culture?
2. When was the last time you made small talk with someone? What did you talk about?
3. Are you good at making small talk, or do you find it difficult to make small talk with strangers?

Conversation ① *Making Small Talk about General Topics*

Track 07

A The weather, jobs, and hobbies are generally considered safe topics for small talk. This is a conversation between two strangers waiting for an elevator. Listen and practice the conversation with a partner.

Chen and Lorena are strangers who happen to be waiting for the same elevator.

Chen   It's really hot today, isn't it?

Lorena It sure is.

Chen   It must be 95 degrees outside.

Lorena I don't mind it. I'm from a hot country.

Chen   Where are you from?

Lorena I'm from Costa Rica. How about you?

Chen   I'm from China.

Lorena Is it hot where you're from?

Chen   Only in the summer. It's quite cold in the winter. Do you work in this building?

Lorena Yes. I work at the dental clinic on the 5th floor. How about you?

Chen   I work at the law office on the 9th floor. May I ask your name?

Lorena I'm Lorena.

Chen   It's nice to meet you, Lorena. I'm Chen.

Lorena Nice meeting you too, Chen.

⊘ **Words to Know**   degree   dental clinic   law office

B Practice the conversation with a partner. Use the information in the box below.

A It's really ¹ .... today, isn't it?

B No kidding!

A Is it ¹ .... where you're from?

B You bet. I'm from ² .... How about you?

A I'm from ³ .... What do you do?

B I'm a graduate student at the university. And you?

A I'm a ⁴ ....

1	2	3	4
cold	Buffalo, New York	Incheon, South Korea	public school teacher
humid	New Orleans, Louisiana	Bangkok, Thailand	computer programmer
hot	Miami, Florida	Sao Paulo, Brazil	doctor

Language Focus

A English speakers often change obvious statements into tag questions when they want to start small talk with people. Look at the chart.

Obvious Statements	Tag Questions
It's hot today.	It's hot today, isn't it?
Lady Gaga sings well.	Lady Gaga sings well, doesn't she?
This is very expensive.	This is very expensive, isn't it?
That hamburger tasted good.	That hamburger tasted good, didn't it?
It was a scary movie.	It was a scary movie, wasn't it?

B Change the obvious statements into tag questions. Write your own obvious statement on line number 6 and then change it into a tag question.

1. The weather is nice. ⇒ ....

2. This is a fun party. ⇒ ....

3. The traffic was bad this morning. ⇒ ....

4. The Toronto Raptors are great this year. ⇒ ....

5. People love BTS. ⇒ ....

6. .... ⇒ ....

Speak Out | Class Activity

Make small talk with a classmate by using the topics below and tag questions. Write your tag questions in the right column first.

a popular singer	IU has a great voice, doesn't she?
a recent movie	
the weather	
a restaurant	
an athlete	

A IU has a great voice, doesn't she?
B I totally agree. I love her voice!

Conversation ② *Making Small Talk at Parties*

◉ Track 08

A Americans love to throw and attend parties. This is a conversation between two strangers who happen to be standing next to each other at a house party. Why do you think the woman strikes up a conversation with the man? Listen and practice the conversation with a partner.

Stephanie and Pedro are strangers who happen to be standing next to each other at a party.

Stephanie Isn't this a great house party?

Pedro Definitely! How do you know the host, Jorge?

Stephanie I don't actually know him. I came here with my roommate. How do you know him?

Pedro We play soccer together on weekends.

Stephanie His parties aren't always this big, are they?

Pedro They are. He loves to throw big, crazy parties.
        I bet he doesn't even know half of the people here.

Stephanie He must be a cool guy.

Pedro He is. I'll introduce you to him later.

Stephanie Thanks.

Pedro Have you tried the mojitos?

Stephanie No, I haven't.

Pedro Jorge's Cuban, so he makes the best mojitos. Let's get some.

Stephanie Okay. I'd love to!

⊘ **Words to Know** host roommate throw

B Practice the conversation with a partner. Use the information in the box below.

A Isn't this a great ¹ _____ ?

B It sure is. How do you know the host?

A She's my ² _____ .

B Cool. Have you tried the ³ _____ ?

A No, not yet.

B It's ⁴ _____ . Let's get some.

A Okay. I'd like that.

1	2	3	4
birthday party	friend	birthday cake	wonderful
graduation party	cousin	chips and salsa	delicious
cocktail party	coworker	salmon	amazing

Language Focus

A English speakers often phrase obvious statements in the form of negative questions when they want to start small talk with people. Look at the chart.

Obvious Statements	Negative Questions
This party is great.	*Isn't this a great party?*
That was a great baseball game.	*Wasn't that a great baseball game?*
He is funny.	*Isn't he funny?*
I love cool autumn days.	*Don't you love cool autumn days?*
She enjoyed living in Paris.	*Didn't she enjoy living in Paris?*

B Change the obvious statements into negative questions. Write your own obvious statement on line number 6 and then change it into a negative question.

1. The concert was loud. ➡ ....

2. This wedding is fun. ➡ ....

3. The Lakers played well. ➡ ....

4. It is cold. ➡ ....

5. I loved the movie. ➡ ....

6. .... ➡ ....

Speak Out | Pair Work

Use your negative question from number 6 in the previous activity to start a conversation with a partner. Then, try to keep the conversation going as long as possible. Once you have finished, switch roles and use your partner's negative question from number 6.

A *Isn't learning English difficult?*
B *Yes, it is.*
A *What do you think the most difficult part is?*
B *I think grammar is the hardest part. I make a lot of grammar mistakes when I speak English.*
A *That's okay. I think that's normal. A lot of English language learners feel that way.*

Conversation 3 *Making Small Talk When in Line*

Track 09

A   It is common to see American people talking to strangers while they are in line at the supermarket. This is a conversation between two strangers in a grocery store checkout line. Listen and practice the conversation with a partner.

Sam and Priya are strangers who happen to be waiting in the same line at the supermarket.

Sam   Excuse me, but could you tell me what time it is?

Priya   Sure. It's 4:35.

Sam   I thought I'd be in and out of the store in ten minutes, but I've been waiting in the checkout line for more than 15 minutes.

Priya   Me, too.

Sam   I noticed you have an accent. May I ask where you're from?

Priya   Of course. I'm from Thailand.

Sam   Isn't it hard to find Thai food here?

Priya   Yes, but I usually substitute Thai ingredients with ones I can find here in the States.

Sam   Can you give me an example?

Priya   Sure. My husband loves spicy papaya salad, but good papaya is impossible to find, so I substitute it with apple.

Sam   Oh, that's clever.

⊘ Words to Know   checkout line   accent   substitute

B   Practice the conversation with a partner. Use the information in the box below.

A   Excuse me, but could you tell me what time it is?

B   Sure. It's ¹ _____ .

A   The lines here are always so long, aren't they?

B   ² _____ ! May I ask where you're from?

A   I'm from ³ _____ .

B   Don't you have a hard time finding food from your country in American supermarkets?

A   ⁴ _____ .

1	2	3	4
2:30	I know	South Korea	I sure do
5:00	You've got that right	Germany	Definitely
9:30	Yeah	Chile	Absolutely

Language Focus

A **English speakers use embedded questions to make requests or questions less direct and more polite. Look at the chart.**

Direct Questions	Embedded Questions
What is your name?	Could you tell me what your name is?
Where are you from?	May I ask where you're from?
Why are you buying a new car?	Do you mind telling me why you are buying a new car?
Where is the costume party?	Do you know where the costume party is?

B **Change the direct questions into embedded questions.**

1. When does the game start? ➡ ....

2. Where can I find cheap apples? ➡ ....

3. How long have you lived here? ➡ ....

4. What kind of food do you like? ➡ ....

5. Why are you studying English? ➡ ....

6. What is the problem? ➡ ....

Speak Out | Pair Work

Look at the underlined direct questions and change them into embedded questions. Then, practice the conversation with a partner.

(Two strangers are waiting in line at the supermarket.)

A Excuse me. ¹Where's the back of the checkout line? ➡

B It's right here behind me.

A Thanks. The lines are always long, aren't they?

B You're right. ²Where are you from? ➡

A I'm from Dallas, Texas. How about you?

B I'm a native of New York.

A Great. ³What time is it? ➡

B It's 4:45 p.m.

A Oh, no. I told my wife I'd be home by 5:00 p.m.

B Since you only have a few items, you can go in front of me.

A Thanks a lot!

Wrap It Up

Vocabulary Check   Match the words with their correct definitions.

1. degrees •
2. roommate •
3. host •
4. accent •
5. substitute •

• ⓐ a person who is having a party at his or her house

• ⓑ a specific group's pronunciation or intonation of words

• ⓒ a measurement of temperature

• ⓓ to take the place of another

• ⓔ someone who lives with you and pays half the rent

Situation Talk

A   **Read the conversation and change the sentences in bold into the types of questions shown in parentheses. After that, practice the conversation with a partner.**

A ¹**It is cold.** (➡ tag question)

B I don't mind the cold. It gets cold in winter in my country.

A ²**Where are you from?** (➡ embedded question)

B I'm from a small town in eastern Canada.

A ³**Do you miss it?** (➡ negative question)

B Sometimes, but I like living in London, too.

A ⁴**Living in London is fun.** (➡ tag question)

B Yeah. There is lots to do here, and I love the London subway system.

A ⁵**Driving everywhere is annoying.** (➡ negative question)

B You've got that right!

B   **Role-play the following situation with a partner.**

Role **A**	Role **B**
You are waiting for an elevator when you notice someone standing next to you. Make small talk with the person while you wait for the elevator.	*When you arrive at the elevators in the building, someone is already standing there.*
1. Make a comment about the weather. 2. Ask the person where he or she is from. 3. Say where you are from and mention how the elevators in this building are always slow.	1. Reply to the person's comment about the weather. 2. Say where you are from and ask the person where he or she is from. 3. Agree with the person that the elevators in this building are very slow.

Proper Small Talk Topics

Track 10

Small talk should always remain positive. That's why it's called small talk and not big talk or deep talk. Small talk should only cover topics that everyone is comfortable discussing. For example, it would be very inappropriate to discuss a marital problem with a stranger because it would only result in making the other person feel uncomfortable. That kind of topic, and similarly sensitive ones, should only be discussed with family members or close friends.

If, by any chance, you had some very good news, such as you received a large raise or received a substantial amount of money for some reason, it would also be inappropriate to share that information with a mere stranger or acquaintance. Topics about personal finances should only be discussed with family members or close friends.

After living in the United States for a time, you may notice that some Americans are "over-sharers," especially when alcohol is involved. When this happens, it is best to nod politely and to excuse yourself from the conversation. You do not want to be on the receiving end of an overly personal conversation with a stranger.

Lastly, the best advice you can follow regarding small talk in America is that you should never discuss politics and religion with people you do not know well. Nothing gets Americans more heated and upset than those two topics. The United States is a country with deep political divides and has people with strong religious views. These topics are often deeply personal for people. It is best to avoid them when making small talk with strangers.

Read the article. Answer these questions.

1. What is an example of an inappropriate small talk topic in American English?
2. What kinds of topics should be discussed with only friends and family members?
3. Why should topics like politics and religion be avoided?

Unit
03

Sit-down
Restaurants

Tipping: What's the Deal?

Although tipping etiquette in the United States can be quite confusing to outside visitors, there are some general guidelines one can follow in order to avoid embarrassing situations while dining out in the country. When food is ordered at a counter or through a drive-thru window, Americans do not feel the need to tip the workers. Sit-down restaurants, however, are in a different category because the food is prepared by professional chefs and delivered by a wait staff. Americans feel obligated to leave a gratuity at these establishments.

Discuss the following questions.

1. How often do you eat at restaurants in your country?
2. When was the last time you went to a restaurant? What did you eat there?
3. Are you expected to leave tips at restaurants in your country? Have you ever left a tip for a server at a restaurant? If you said yes, how much did you tip?

If the food and the service are good, a tip between 15% and 20% of the pretax total is customary. If the service is outstanding, you can tip 25% or higher. Some Americans enjoy over-tipping because they know how difficult being a server can be. Servers spend most of their shifts on their feet shuffling back and forth between the kitchen and the customers' tables. They also understand that servers in restaurants need tips to survive. Some Americans feel the responsibility to leave at least a 15% to 20% tip, despite poor service, although they might still decide to make a complaint to the manager.

Track 12

A Once you are ready to order, it is okay to make eye contact with your server and to slightly raise your hand in order to signal that you are ready to order. This is a conversation between a waitress and a customer. Listen and practice the conversation with a partner.

John has signaled to the waitress that he and his wife are ready to order.

Waitress	Are you ready to order?
John	Yes, we're ready. Thanks. I will have the rib-eye steak with a baked potato.
Waitress	How do you want your steak?
John	Medium.
Waitress	Okay. Anything to drink with that?
John	A Diet Coke. And my wife will have the grilled chicken with a side of French fries and a Sprite.
Waitress	Okay, so that's one rib-eye with a baked potato and a Diet Coke, and one order of grilled chicken with a side of fries and a Diet Sprite?
John	Not Diet Sprite. Just a regular Sprite.
Waitress	Oh, I'm sorry. One Diet Coke and one regular Sprite.
John	That's correct.
Waitress	I'll be back shortly with your drinks.

⊘ **Words to Know** baked grilled side

B Practice the conversation with a partner. Use the information in the box below.

A ¹ _____ ?

B ² _____ the steak.

A What side would you like with that?

B I'll have the ³ _____ .

A Anything to drink?

B Yes. I'll have a ⁴ _____ .

A I'll be right back with your drink.

1	2	3	4
Can I take your order	I'll have	French fries	Coke
Are you ready to order	I want	salad	glass of red wine
What can I get for you today	I'd like	baked potato	sparkling water

Language Focus

A There are several expressions Americans can use when taking orders or ordering food at a restaurant. Look at the chart.

Taking an Order	Ordering Food
Are you ready to order?	I'll have the T-bone steak.
Can/May I take your order?	I'd like a cheeseburger, French fries, and a Coke.
What can I get for you today?	I want a sausage and cheese omelet.
What would you like to order?	Can I get a large pepperoni pizza?

B Fill in the blanks by using the expressions in the chart for ordering food and taking orders. Then, practice the conversations with a partner.

1. A What can I get for you today?

   B _____ the grilled salmon.

2. A _____ ?

   B I'd like the broccoli soup and a club sandwich.

3. A Anything to drink?

   B Yes, _____ a Diet Coke.

4. A _____ ?

   B _____ a cheeseburger and French fries.

Speak Out | Pair Work

Look at the menu. Then, practice taking orders and ordering food. Take turns being a server and a customer.

Main Courses		Sides		Drinks		Desserts	
Grilled Chicken	13.99	Baked Potato	3.99	Soda	0.99	Chocolate Cake	2.75
New York Steak	15.99	French Fries	3.50	Juice	1.99	Apple Pie	2.50
Hamburger	9.99	Garden Salad	3.99	Sparkling Water	1.99	Ice Cream	2.00

A *What can I get for you today?*

B *I'd like a New York steak, a baked potato, and some juice.*

A *Would you like anything for dessert?*

B *Yes. I'd like a piece of apple pie.*

Conversation ② Asking for the Check

A   When you are finished with your meal, you should get the server's attention and ask for the check. Americans tip their waiters or waitresses for providing services when paying the check. Listen and practice the conversation with a partner.

A couple has finished eating, and they are now asking for the check.

John   Excuse me, miss.

Waitress Yes. Is there anything else I can get for you?

John   No, thank you. Just the check, please.

Waitress Of course. Here you are.

John   Do you accept credit cards?

Waitress Yes. We accept all major credit cards.

John   I can't read this total. Does this say $59.95?

Waitress No, sir. It says $39.95.

John   Oh, okay. Here's my card.

Waitress I'll be right back with your receipt.

John   *(To his wife)* She was very nice. I'm going to leave ten dollars for the tip.

⊘ **Words to Know**   check   credit card   receipt   tip

B   Practice the conversation with a partner. Use the information in the box below.

A   ¹ _____ ?

B   No, thank you. Just the ² _____ , please.

A   Of course. Here you are.

B   Do you accept credit cards?

A   Yes. We accept all major credit cards.

B   Okay. Here's my card.

A   I'll be right back with your receipt.

B   *(To your company)* The service was ³ _____ . I'll tip her ⁴ _____ .

1	2	3	4
Would you like anything else	check	excellent	$20
Can I get you some dessert	bill	good	$10
Is there anything else I can get for you	damage (slang)	not bad	$5

Language Focus

A Look at the chart that shows the standard tip amounts based on the quality of service.

Quality of Service	Tip Percentage
okay / average / not bad	15%
good / great / first-rate	20%
wonderful / excellent / fantastic	25%
amazing / the best ever	25%+

B Read the pre-tip totals and comments. Then, choose the best matching totals including tips. Use the chart to help you.

	Pre-tip Totals	Comments	Totals Including Tips
1.	$50.00	"I thought the server did a good job."	
2.	$32.89	"The service wasn't bad."	
3.	$59.00	"She was the best server ever!"	
4.	$20.00	"The service was excellent in my opinion."	
5.	$15.00	"In my opinion, the service was average."	

ⓐ $25.00
ⓑ $18.00
ⓒ $60.00
ⓓ $37.84
ⓔ $77.00

Speak Out | Pair Work

Find a partner. Then, read about and discuss the people's dining experiences below and decide on appropriate tip amounts based on their experiences. When you and your partner agree on a tip amount, write it on the receipt where it reads *Tip Amount*.

Golden State Restaurant
San Francisco, CA
(415) 393-0874
Sale
Steak Sandwich
French Fries
Coke
Total: $32.59

Tip Amount: ....

John: *The food and the service were excellent. My food arrived on time, and the waitress was very friendly.*

The Good Morning Bistro
Buffalo, NY
(628) 585-4875
Sale
Cheeseburger
Cobb Salad
Lemonade
Total: $17.50

Tip Amount: ....

Sarah: *My cheeseburger and salad were very delicious, but it took almost 40 minutes for me to get my food. The server also forgot my lemonade.*

Jacob's Pizzeria
Hugo, MN
(651) 997-4234
Sale
Pan Pizza
Garlic Bread
Diet Coke
Total: $22.99

Tip Amount: ....

Alyssa: *The pizza was amazing. It was the best I've ever had! The server was also super nice. I will definitely come back.*

A *How much of a tip should he give?*

B *I think it is appropriate to tip $7.*

Conversation ③ Customers with Special Diets

Track 14

A There are vegetarian, vegan, and other options available at many American restaurants these days. Do you or anyone you know follow a vegetarian, vegan, pescatarian, or ketogenic diet? Listen and practice the conversation with a partner.

Laurel is asking the waiter about the restaurant's vegan and vegetarian options.

Waiter Are you ready to order?

Laurel Actually, we were wondering if there are any vegetarian options on your menu. We don't see any.

Waiter If you look on the back page of the menu, you'll find several vegetarian options.

Laurel Oh, here they are. Hmm, I think I'll have the vegan pasta, and my friend will have the vegetarian lasagna. I'm vegan, but she eats dairy.

Waiter I see. Would you like anything to drink?

Laurel We'd really like to split a bottle of wine. What do you recommend?

Waiter I highly recommend the Pinot Noir. I think it will go nicely with your pasta dishes.

Laurel Let's do that.

Waiter I'll be right back with your bottle of wine.

Laurel Thank you.

⊘ **Words to Know**   vegan   vegetarian   dairy   split

B Practice the conversation with a partner. Use the information in the box below.

A Are you ready to order?

B Do you have any ¹ _____ options?

A There are several on ² _____ .

B Here they are. I think I'll have the ³ _____ , and my friend will have the vegetarian lasagna.

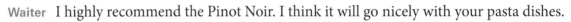

1	2	3
vegetarian	the back page of the menu	vegetarian pizza
vegan	this menu	vegan pasta
non-meat	this side of the menu	tofu salad

Language Focus

A   A lot of Americans have special food preferences or follow special diets. Here is some information about a few of the special diets that are popular in the United States right now.

Vegetarian Diet	Vegan Diet	Pescatarian Diet	Ketogenic Diet
a plant-based diet which includes some dairy products and eggs	a plant-based diet which excludes all dairy and eggs	a plant and fish-based diet which excludes meat such as pork, chicken, and beef	a diet very low in carbohydrates but high in protein and fats

B   Write the appropriate diet names from the chart above in the blanks.

1. I'm sorry, but do you have any _____ options? I don't eat any meat or dairy.

2. Excuse me, miss. Does your restaurant serve fish? I'm a _____ .

3. I follow the _____ diet, so I'd like the steak with a side salad instead of a baked potato. I'd like the side salad without dressing, too.

4. A Do you have a _____ menu?

    B We have several salad dishes right here. Do you eat eggs?

    A Yes. Eggs are okay.

Speak Out | Pair Work

Create your own specialty menu with dishes that would be suitable for a customer who follows one of these four diets: vegetarian, vegan, pescatarian, or ketogenic. Then, change books with a partner and role-play a conversation between a customer and a server by using each other's menus.

SPECIAL MENU

Main Courses		Sides	
1.	$	1.	$
2.	$	2.	$
3.	$	3.	$

Drinks		Desserts	
1.	$	1.	$
2.	$	2.	$
3.	$	3.	$

A *Are you ready to order?*

B *I don't eat meat, eggs, or dairy, so I'll have the tofu salad.*

Wrap It Up

Vocabulary Check Fill in the blanks with the correct answers.

1. The _____ potato just came out of the oven.   ⓐ grilled   ⓑ baked

2. I'm going to leave ten dollars for the _____.   ⓐ menu   ⓑ tip

3. Would you like to keep the _____ ?   ⓐ receipt   ⓑ credit card

4. Let's _____ a bottle of wine.   ⓐ accept   ⓑ split

5. Maria's a _____. She eats eggs and dairy, but not any meat.

                                                    ⓐ vegetarian   ⓑ vegan

Situation Talk

A   **Role-play the following situation with a partner.**

Role **A**	Role **B**
You are a server, and a customer has just sat down in your section.	*You have just sat down to eat in your favorite hamburger restaurant.*
1. Greet the customer and ask him or her if he or she is ready to order.	1. Say yes and order a cheeseburger and French fries.
2. Ask the customer if he or she would like anything to drink.	2. Say you would like a Diet Coke.
3. Tell the customer you will be right back with his or her drink.	3. Say "Thank you." to the server.

B   **Find a partner and agree to pay for the meals below on customer A's credit card. Fill out the credit card receipt together by deciding on an appropriate tip amount based on both of your dining experiences. Don't forget to have customer A sign the receipt!**

Customer A		Customer B
	**BIG LAKE BURGERS** **ST. PAUL, MN** (612) 508-7044 Sale Credit Card # 8979344843527569	
Club Sandwich with Fries: $13.99	Amount: $ _____	Deluxe Cheeseburger with Fries: $11.99
Opinion: *You thought the server was polite, but the bread on your sandwich was stale. The French fries tasted good, but the server brought you the wrong drink. She quickly corrected the mistake.*	Tip: $ _____ Total: $ _____ Signature _____	**Opinion**: *You thought the service was pretty good. You waited 20 minutes for your meal. It was cooked properly, and the server was polite, but she never offered to refill your Coke during your time there.*

When and Where Do I Tip?

Track 15

Tipping in the United States is not only confusing when it comes to eating in restaurants. There are other situations where tipping is expected. For example, there are several situations in which tipping is appropriate at hotels. If a bellhop carries your bags to your room, you are expected to give him or her one dollar per bag or perhaps two if the hotel is very nice. Once the bellhop has placed your bags in the room, he or she will pause for a moment. This is the time to give him or her the tip.

If you order room service at the hotel, expect to tip 20 percent of the pretax total for the meal. Since room service is usually paid for by credit or debit card, you can write in the tip amount where it reads "Tip" or "Gratuity." Housekeeping staff members also expect a tip for cleaning your room. At most hotels, it is appropriate to leave $2 for the maid; however, in very nice hotels, $3 to $5 is expected. You can usually find a tray with business cards for the hotel on a desk in the hotel room. You can leave the maid a tip by placing the money in this tray.

Now, let's talk about tipping in regard to taxis or ride-sharing apps such as Uber and Lyft. If you are taking

a taxi in the United States, the appropriate tip amount is between 15% and 20% of the fare, assuming the service was adequate. It is always a good idea to have several one-dollar bills in your wallet or purse in cases like these. If your taxi fare is $10, you can simply hand the driver the fare amount and two extra dollars. If your fare is $16, give the driver $20 and say "Keep the change." If you are using a ride-sharing app, pay the fare through the app itself. You can then tip by using cash. 15% to 20% is typical, or you can provide a tip for the driver within the app itself.

Read the article. Check T for true or F for false.

1. Tipping in America is only necessary in restaurants.   T ☐ / F ☐
2. One or two dollars is an appropriate tip for housekeeping at a hotel.   T ☐ / F ☐
3. The appropriate tip amount for a taxi driver is between 15% and 20%.   T ☐ / F ☐

A Shopper's Paradise

Discuss the following questions.

1. How often do you go shopping in your country?
2. What kinds of items do you enjoy shopping for? Clothes, food, electronics, etc.?
3. Which kind of shopping do you prefer, online or offline? Why?

Track 16

Places to Shop in America

The United States is home to a variety of shopping centers. Supermarkets are probably the most popular these days because they offer everything you need under one roof. Although the prices are typically low at these places, the quality of the products can also be subpar.

Although malls are also places where you can do your shopping under one roof, the shops in these places are separately owned businesses. In malls, you can find brand-name clothes and apparel, but they are not usually sold at discounts. Outlet malls, unlike traditional malls, mainly focus on selling clothes at significant discounts. These places are less luxurious than regular malls; however, you can find the previous season's fashions for up to 70% off or more.

Thrift stores are stores that sell used clothes and other items. One of the most popular thrift stores in the United States is Goodwill. There, items are separated into different departments just like at a regular store. The only difference is that the items have been donated by do-gooders and are now being resold. Goodwill uses the money it earns to help disadvantaged people.

A garage sale, on the other hand, usually takes place in the garage or front yard of a person's house. The items for sale at a garage sale usually come from a family who is looking to get rid of items they do not use. Good bargains can be found at a garage sale, and it is one of the rare occasions where bargaining for a lower price is appropriate in America.

Conversation ❶ At a Clothing Store

A Americans don't like workers in clothes shops to stand near them. If they need assistance, they will ask a worker for help. This is a conversation between a shopper and a worker at a clothing store. Listen and practice the conversation with a partner.

Clara is shopping for jeans and asks the sales clerk for assistance.

Clara	Excuse me, miss. Could I have some assistance?
Sales Clerk	Of course. How can I help you?
Clara	I was wondering if you have these jeans in black with a 28-inch waist.
Sales Clerk	Let me check. Here you are. Why don't you try them on? Our fitting rooms are right over there.

(moments later)

Clara	What do you think about the length?
Sales Clerk	The length is fine, but they're a little snug around the waistline. May I recommend a 30? This brand tends to run small.
Clara	Okay.
Sales Clerk	Here's a pair with a 30-inch waist. Try these on.

(moments later)

Clara	These feel much more comfortable.
Sales Clerk	And they fit you perfectly around the hips. They look great.
Clara	I'll take them.

✅ Words to Know   assistance   snug   fit

B Practice the conversation with a partner. Use the information in the box below.

A What do you think about the ¹_____?

B It's okay, but they're a little ²_____ around the waistline. May I recommend a 30? This brand tends to run ³_____.

A Okay.

B Here's a pair with a 30-inch-waist size. Try these on.

1	2	3
length	snug	small
color	loose	large
shape	tight	skintight

Language Focus

A **Look at the words that describe different types of fits in clothes.**

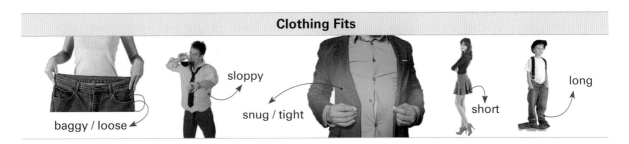

Clothing Fits

baggy / loose · sloppy · snug / tight · short · long

B **Fill in the blanks by using the words in the chart above.**

1. These pants are too _____. The bottoms are touching the floor!

2. Sarah's mom thinks her daughter's skirt is inappropriate. She believes it is too _____.

3. These pants are too _____. I can't even breathe!

4. I bought XL shorts, but I should have bought L because they're too _____.

5. Juyeon's boyfriend is a _____ dresser. His shirts are never tucked in, his pants have food stains on them, and his clothes don't fit him properly.

Speak Out

A **Look at the people in the pictures. Then, describe their clothing.**

April

Brian

Justine

April is wearing tight, green pants and …

B **What are your style preferences? Say how you like to wear your jeans, shirts, jackets, etc.**

I like to wear loose shirts and tight jeans.

Conversation ② *At a Garage Sale*

A Americans love bargains. Thrift stores and garage sales are excellent places to find good bargains. Although prices at thrift stores are fixed, it is acceptable to negotiate for lower prices on items at garage sales. This is a conversation between a buyer and a seller at a garage sale. Listen and practice the conversation with a partner.

Mark is bargaining for a used fan at Kristie's garage sale.

Mark   Does this fan work well?

Kristie Yes, it works very well.

Mark   How much do you want for it?

Kristie We're asking $25 for it. It's only two years old.

Mark   Would you be willing to sell it for $10?

Kristie I'm sorry, but I can't go that low.

Mark   How about $15?

Kristie I really wanted to get at least $25 for it.

Mark   Why don't we meet halfway? I'll go up five dollars, and you come down five dollars.

Kristie Okay, deal.

Mark   Great! Here's twenty dollars.

⊙ Words to Know   bargain   at least   halfway   deal

B Practice the conversation with a partner. Use the information in the box below.

A ¹ _____ for this espresso maker?

B ² _____ $25 for it. It's only a year old.

A Would you be willing to sell it for $15?

B I'm sorry, but we can't ³ _____ .

A How about $20?

B Okay, ⁴ _____ .

1	2	3	4
How much do you want	We're asking	go that low	deal
How much are you asking	We're looking for	do it for that	you've got a deal
How much would you like	We'd like	agree to that	we can do it for that

Language Focus

A   There are several expressions we can use when bargaining. Look at the chart.

Making an Offer	Rejecting an Offer
How about $50 for it?	I'm sorry, but I can't do it for $50.
Would you consider taking $300 for it?	I'm sorry, but $300 is too low.
Can/Could I offer you $75 for it?	$75? No, that's too low.
Would you take $5 for it?	Are you kidding me? (strong rejection / slightly impolite)
Would you be willing to sell it for $10?	That's ridiculous. (strong rejection / impolite)

B   Fill in the blanks with offers or rejections by using some of the expressions in the chart.

1.   Can I offer you $35 for it?

2.   I'm sorry, but I can't do it for $70.

3.   Would you take $10 for it?

4. $100? Are you kidding me? It's worth twice that!

5.   How about $5 for it?

Speak Out | Pair Work

Find a partner. Then, imagine you are at a garage sale. Bargain for a better price for the items on the list. Reject your partner's first offer, but accept your partner's second offer.

Items for Sale

$45 $80 $15 $20 $5 $25

A   *How about $30 for this cordless drill?*
B   *$30? No, I can't do it for that price.*
A   *Would you sell it for $35?*
B   *Okay, deal.*

Track 19

A Americans love shopping at supermarkets because supermarkets offer the widest array of products under one roof, and the prices are very competitive. This is a conversation between a customer and a sales clerk at a supermarket. Listen and practice the conversation with a partner.

Alicia asks a sales clerk where some items on her list are located in the supermarket.

Alicia	Excuse me. Do you work here?
Sales Clerk	Yes, I do. How can I help you?
Alicia	I'm looking for olive oil, but I can't seem to find it.
Sales Clerk	Olive oil is in aisle number 6. That is the condiments, sauces, and spices aisle.
Alicia	Oh, I must have missed it. Thank you. Could you also tell me where the electronics department is? I heard that you are having a sale on wireless earphones.
Sales Clerk	Yes, we are. The electronics department is next to housewares and across from menswear.
Alicia	Could you point me in the right direction?
Sales Clerk	Sure. Go straight and turn right. Then, go past housewares until you see menswear on your right and the electronics department on your left.
Alicia	Great. Thank you so much for your help.
Sales Clerk	It's my pleasure.

⊘ Words to Know   aisle   condiments   housewares

B Practice the conversation with a partner. Use the information in the box below.

A Excuse me. ¹_____?

B Yes. How can I help you?

A ²_____ olive oil, but I can't seem to find it.

B Olive oil is in aisle 6. That is the condiments, sauces, and spices aisle.

A Oh, ³_____. Thank you. Could you also tell me where the hardware department is?

B The hardware depertment is ⁴_____ housewares.

1	2	3	4
Do you work here	I'm looking for	I must have missed it	next to
Can you help me	I'm trying to find	I guess I walked right past it	across from
Can I get some assistance	I'm searching for	I didn't see it	near

Language Focus

A When visiting a large supermarket, you might find it necessary to ask for directions. Look at some prepositions which tell where things are located.

Prepositions of Place

in front of   behind   across from   next to   between   near

B Look at the map and write the appropriate prepositions in the blanks.

1. The coffee shop is .... the restaurant and the bakery.

2. The clothing store is .... the bookstore.

3. The bookstore is .... the pet shop.

4. The restaurant is .... the park.

Speak Out | Pair Work

Find a partner. Then, ask for and give directions to different departments in the supermarket by looking at the map. Use some of the prepositions from the chart above when necessary.

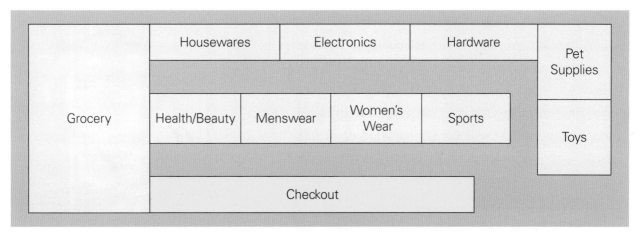

A *Excuse me. Could you tell me where the hardware department is?*

B *It's between the electronics and pet supplies departments. And it's across from the sports section.*

Wrap It Up

Complete the sentences by using the words in the box.

aisle	condiments	deal	halfway	snug

1. These pants feel too tight. They're too _____ in the waist.

2. Let's make a _____. If you give me your bicycle, I will give you my scooter.

3. I want to pay five dollars, and you want 15 dollars. Let's meet _____ at 10 dollars.

4. I don't like adding any _____ like ketchup or mustard to my hot dog.

5. Attention! Clean up on _____ number 3!

Situation Talk

A   **Role-play the following situation with a partner.**

Role A	Role B
You want to buy a computer printer at a garage sale.	*You are selling items at a garage sale.*
1. Ask B how much the printer costs. 2. Tell B it is kind of old. Offer him or her $30. 3. Ask B to meet halfway. Offer him or her $35.	1. Say you are selling it for $50. 2. Say you can't sell it for that price. Tell A that you wanted to get at least $40 for it. It's only one year old. 3. Accept the offer of $35.

B   **Find a partner. Then, draw a floor plan of the floor you are studying on right now. When you have finished drawing the map together, ask for and give directions to different classrooms, offices, and other rooms on the floor.**

A   *Where is the men's restroom?*

B   *It's between the women's restroom and the stairs. It's also across from the elevators.*

Can I Return This?

Track 20

Most large chain stores in the United States will let you return an item as long as you have the receipt. The main reason large stores in the U.S. have such friendly return policies is that they want to keep their customers happy. Returning items at smaller boutiques or individually owned shops can be more difficult depending on each store's return policy. At large chains, though, returning items is a relatively easy process.

First, you must find the area in the store named "Customer Service Center," "Customer Returns," or just "Returns." Each store might have a slightly different name, but the function of the department is the same. Once you have found the returns department, get in line and wait your turn. When it is your turn to return the item, present the item you want to return, in its original packaging if possible, and the receipt.

The customer service representative may ask you why you want to return it. If the item isn't working properly or the clothing does not fit you properly, you can give the person that information. You can also simply say that you decided you did not want the item any longer or that you changed your mind about the purchase.

The customer service representative will then ask you if you want a cash refund or the money returned to your credit card if you used that method of payment. You might even be given the option of store credit. You should inform the representative which option you prefer. The entire return process is that easy.

Now, some people will argue that these policies result in abuse. They say customers buy items, use them until they no longer need them, and then return them. It is true that people do this, but remember that abuse of the system hurts everyone because corporations must raise prices to offset their losses. So it is best to return an item only when you truly have not used it yet, or it does not work or fit properly.

Read the article. Answer these questions.
1. What do you need in order to return an item at most large chain stores?
2. What should you do if you want a cash refund for an item?
3. How does abuse of a store's return policy hurt all of the customers?

Let's Party!

Track 21

Americans Like to Have Parties

If baseball is considered the national pastime in America, then going to parties may be a close second. Parties vary from lavish events where guests wear tuxedoes and gowns to house parties where guests wear jeans and T-shirts. There are so many kinds of parties that it would be impossible to make a comprehensive list; however, here are a few examples of some common types of parties in the United States.

A dinner party is a low-key event where a host or hosts invite friends or family members to their homes for a meal. When attending a dinner party, it is a good idea to bring a bottle of wine. A $15 to $20 bottle is acceptable. It shows your gratitude to the host. It is also common to compliment the host on the food.

Discuss the following questions.

1. Have you ever been to a dinner party? If yes, how was it? Did you bring anything to the party?
2. What kinds of office parties do companies have in your country? Do companies have holiday office parties? If yes, what holidays do they celebrate?
3. Have you ever been to a cocktail party? If yes, what was the reason for the cocktail party?

A house party is different than a dinner party as more guests are invited, and the emphasis is less on the food and more on the alcohol. Most university students enjoy house parties because they can meet people and drink large quantities of alcohol for very little money.

Office Christmas parties are often held on the last day of work before Christmas vacation begins. A Christmas party may take place at an office, a bar, or a restaurant where food and alcoholic beverages are served. Oftentimes, a few workers get too drunk and embarrass themselves. This can lead to unnecessary drama in the workplace when everyone returns from vacation.

Conversation ❶ At a Dinner Party

🔊Track 22

A Those who find themselves spending a substantial amount of time in the United States will at one time or another be invited to a dinner party. This is a conversation between a guest and a host at a dinner party. Listen and practice the conversation with a partner.

Hyejin is a guest at Molly's dinner party.

Hyejin These dinner rolls are really delicious, Molly!

Molly Thank you. I used my grandmother's recipe.

Hyejin Did your grandmother introduce you to baking?

Molly Yes, she did.

Hyejin How old were you when she taught you?

Molly I was really young—maybe four or five. My parents both worked, so I spent a lot of time at my grandparents' house when I was young.

Hyejin Me, too! My grandmother taught me how to make kimchi stew when I was six.

Molly That's so cool. My grandmother and I baked all kinds of bread and cookies.

Hyejin Some of my best memories of my grandmother are of us cooking together.

Molly Same here. Every time I make a batch of my grandmother's cookies, I think about her.

Hyejin That's sweet. Can you pass me the plate of dinner rolls? They're so delicious that I'm going to have another one.

Molly Of course. Enjoy!

⊘ **Words to Know**   recipe   introduce   batch

B Practice the conversation with a partner. Use the information in the box below.

A These ¹ _____ are really delicious, Molly!

B Thank you. I used my grandmother's recipe.

A Did your grandmother introduce you to baking?

B Yes, she did.

A That's sweet. ² _____ me the dinner rolls?

B Sure. ³ _____ !

1	2	3
croissants	Can you pass	Enjoy
buns	Would you mind passing	Bon appetite
muffins	Do you think you could pass	Eat up

Language Focus

A English speakers often phrase requests as questions in order to make them more polite. Look at the chart.

Direct Requests (impolite)	Indirect Requests (polite)
Pass me the fried rice.	*Could you pass me the fried rice?*
Give me a glass.	*Can you give me a glass?*
Make me a sandwich.	*Would you mind making me a sandwich?*
Bake some cookies for us.	*Do you mind baking some cookies for us?*

B Change the direct requests into indirect requests by phrasing them as questions.

1. Pass me the chicken. ➡ _____

2. Bake some muffins for me. ➡ _____

3. Give me a fork. ➡ _____

4. Show us how to do it. ➡ _____

5. Tell me your name. ➡ _____

6. Send me the report via email. ➡ _____

Speak Out | Pair Work

Look at the underlined impolite requests and change them into polite questions. Then, practice the conversation with a partner.

(Sarah and Michelle are at a dinner party.)

A Sarah, ¹pass me the potatoes. ➡ _____

B Here you are, Michelle.

A ²Give me a spoon, too. ➡ _____

B Okay. Here's a spoon.

A The potatoes are very good.

B Thank you. ³Pass me the meatballs. ➡ _____

A Here you are.

B ⁴Give me some ketchup. ➡ _____

A Here's the ketchup.

Conversation ② At a Christmas Party

Track 23

A If you work for an American company, there is a good chance you will get to experience an office Christmas party. Workers sometimes choose to do secret Santa gift exchanges. This involves drawing a name randomly and buying a present for that person. This is a conversation between two colleagues at an office Christmas party. Listen and practice the conversation with a partner.

Simon and Monique are having a conversation at an office Christmas party.

Simon   Are you enjoying the Christmas party, Monique?

Monique   I sure am. How about you, Simon?

Simon   Definitely. Have you tried Rebecca's Russian tea cakes yet?

Monique   No, I haven't.

Simon   You've got to. They're delightful. But you'd better hurry up before they're all gone.

Monique   Okay, I will.

Simon   Who's your secret Santa?

Monique   I can't tell you. It's supposed to be a secret.

Simon   Come on. I'll tell you who mine is.

Monique   All right. My secret Santa is Charles. I got him printed socks with pictures of Rudolph the Red-Nosed Reindeer on them. How about you?

Simon   Actually, you're my secret Santa.

Monique   Really? What did you get me?

Simon   Here you are. It's an engraved pencil set. All the pencils have your name on them.

Monique   Oh, that's so cool. Thank you, Simon!

Words to Know   delightful   be supposed to   engraved

B Practice the conversation with a partner. Use the information in the box below.

A   Have you tried ¹ _____ yet?

B   ² _____ .

A   You ³ _____ . They're really good. But you'd better hurry up before they're all gone.

B   Okay, I will.

1	2	3
Wanda's gingerbread cookies	No, I haven't.	've got to
Dan's peppermint bark	Not yet.	must
Jean's holiday muffins	No.	have to

Language Focus

A Americans tend to use exaggerated language when encouraging others to try something they themselves have enjoyed. Look at some expressions that can be used in order to strongly encourage others to try something.

must	have to / has to	've got to / 's got to
You **must** try this bread!	You **have to** try this bread!	You**'ve got to** try this bread!
She **must** come to the party!	She **has to** come to the party!	She**'s got to** come to the party!
They **must** try the lobster when they visit Maine!	They **have to** try the lobster when they visit Maine!	They**'ve got to** try the lobster when they visit Maine!

B Complete the sentences by using the expressions from the chart.

1. You / taste this soup ➡ *You have to taste this soup!*

2. He / try the pasta ➡

3. They / see the parade ➡

4. You / try this recipe ➡

5. Kelly / come to the Christmas party ➡

6. Minho / go to Disneyland when he visits Orlando

➡

Speak Out | Class Activity

Encourage your classmates to try the food items in the pictures.

① gingerbread cookies
② Christmas cake
③ baked ham
④ mulled wine
⑤ homemade pudding
⑥ roast turkey

Conversation ③ *At a Cocktail Party*

A   A cocktail party in the United States is a more grown-up and sophisticated version of a house party. While house parties are popular with college students and young adults, those who are older and more mature prefer cocktail parties. This is a conversation between two partygoers at a cocktail party. Listen and practice the conversation with a partner.

David and Coral are attending the same cocktail party.

David   What are you drinking?

Coral   It's an orange vodka martini.

David   It looks good.

Coral   You should get one.

David   I'm going to as soon as I finish my scotch and soda.

Coral   How do you know Scott, the host?

David   We used to be college roommates. How do you know him?

Coral   His sister, Beth, is my best friend, so I've known him since he was a child.

David   You've known him longer than I have. What was he like as a child?

Coral   He was kind of a nerd in high school.

David   *(laughing)* That's funny. He isn't a nerd anymore.

Coral   No kidding! He started working out, and now he's so handsome and successful.

David   It's really cool that his company organized this charity event.

Coral   I agree.

⊘ Words to Know   nerd   No kidding!   organize   charity

B   Practice the conversation with a partner. Use the information in the box below.

A   How do you know Ally, the host of the party?

B   We used to ¹ .... How about you?

A   She's ² .... I've known her since ³ ....

B   That's great.

1	2	3
be college roommates	my boss	2016
go to the same gym	my best friend	middle school
belong to the same cycling club	my brother's wife	university

Language Focus

A If you want to discuss something you did regularly in the past but you do not do it now, you can use the phrase "used to." If you did something in the past and you still do it now, you can use the present perfect tense. Look at the chart.

used to *true in the past but untrue now	Tim and Diane **used to** play tennis together. We **used to** live in the same city. Steven **used to** teach English at a university.
Present Perfect Tense **(have + p.p.)** *true in the past and true now	Jackie and Bruce **have played** tennis together since college. They**'ve lived** in the same city since 2013. She **has taught** English at a university for years.

B Make sentences using "used to" or the present perfect tense depending on the given information.

	Past	Now

1. (Minseong and Jiwoo / study English together / 2017) — Yes Yes

   Minseong and Jiwoo have studied English together since 2017.

2. (Holly and Emily / be roommates / in college) — Yes No

3. (We / know each other / elementary school) — Yes Yes

4. (I / work at ABC Company) — Yes No

Speak Out | Pair Work

Make a list of five things you did in the past and check Yes or No depending on whether or not you do them now. Then, share your items with a partner by using "used to" or the present perfect tense.

Past	Now
1. *I played soccer.*	☑ Yes ☐ No
2.	☐ Yes ☐ No
3.	☐ Yes ☐ No
4.	☐ Yes ☐ No
5.	☐ Yes ☐ No

I have played soccer since elementary school.

Wrap It Up

Match the words with their correct definitions.

1. batch •

2. delightful •

3. engraved •

4. introduce •

5. charity •

• ⓐ a nonprofit organization which helps people

• ⓑ having had a design cut into a hard surface

• ⓒ a group of baked goods such as cookies or muffins

• ⓓ wonderful; excellent; charming

• ⓔ to provide someone with an opportunity to learn something

Situation Talk

A **Find a partner. Then, take turns encouraging your partner to try the food and drink items.**

sliders

nachos and salsa

chili dogs

canape

champagne

beer

A *You've got to try this canape. It's delicious!*

B *Okay, I will.*

B **Role-play the following situation with a partner.**

Role A	Role B
You are a guest at a dinner party.	*You are the host of a dinner party.*
1. Say the bread is delicious. 2. Ask B for the bread recipe. 3. Ask B how old he or she was when he or she learned how to bake. 4. Say "That's great." Ask B to pass you some more bread.	1. Say thank you. 2. Say yes. Tell A that it is your grandmother's recipe. 3. Say that you learned how to bake when you were 8 years old and that you and your grandmother have baked all kinds of bread since then. 4. Say sure. Tell A to enjoy the bread because there is lots of it.

College House Parties

Track 25

House parties are a big part of the university experience in the United States. Compared to other countries, the United States has an unusually high minimum drinking age of 21 years old. This means that most university students in America cannot legally drink until their junior year of university.

In reality, a large number of freshmen and sophomore students drink anyway, but they do so at house parties instead of at bars. These parties are also known as keggers. A keg of beer is a large metal barrel consisting of 30 gallons of beer or less. The average house party keg contains 15.5 gallons, or approximately 59 liters of beer. If you attend the party, you can purchase a plastic cup at the door for $5. Once you have purchased your cup, you can fill it up as many times as you would like.

But beware. You are going to have to push and shove your way to the keg because there are going to be a lot of people trying to fill their cups. And these parties do not come without inconveniences. With all of the beer being consumed by partygoers, the lines for the bathrooms are going to be extremely long. In addition, if you are underage, you are committing a crime by drinking alcohol and could be fined by the police if you are stopped and questioned.

beer keg

There are other times when kegs are not available, and the party is known as BYOB, or bring your own beer. In these cases, you should buy the alcohol you want to consume for yourself beforehand. You will not be expected to share your alcohol with others because they will also be bringing their own; however, it is completely acceptable to share your alcohol if you want to.

The most important thing to remember is that you should never drive a car if you are going to be drinking at a party. Walk or use a ride-sharing app or taxi so that you do not find yourself stranded at the party. It is also best to attend these kinds of parties with friends. Planning ahead and using the buddy system is the best way to enjoy yourself at a college party in the United States.

Read the article. Check T for true or F for false.
1. The USA has an unusually high minimum drinking age of 20 years old. T ☐ / F ☐
2. A kegger is a large party where kegs of beer are provided for guests. T ☐ / F ☐
3. At a BYOB party, you will be expected to share your alcohol with others. T ☐ / F ☐

Unit
06

Getting Around Town

🔊 Track 26

Transportation in the USA

The kind of transportation you are most likely to rely on in the United States depends mainly on where you decide to live. If you choose to live in a big city like New York, for example, you will find a vast network of subway trains, buses, and taxis available to residents. Not all big cities in the U.S. have train systems, however, which is why car ownership is so high in the USA. In New York City, most residents choose to walk, take the subway, take a taxi, or ride on the bus. And residents find that they can reach most places in the city in a reasonable amount of time by using these forms of public transportation.

Discuss the following questions.

1. How do you get around the city you live in: by bus, subway, taxi, ridesharing service, or car?
2. Does your city have a good public transportation system? What do you like about it? What don't you like about it?
3. Do you want to own a car? What are the advantages and disadvantages of having a car?

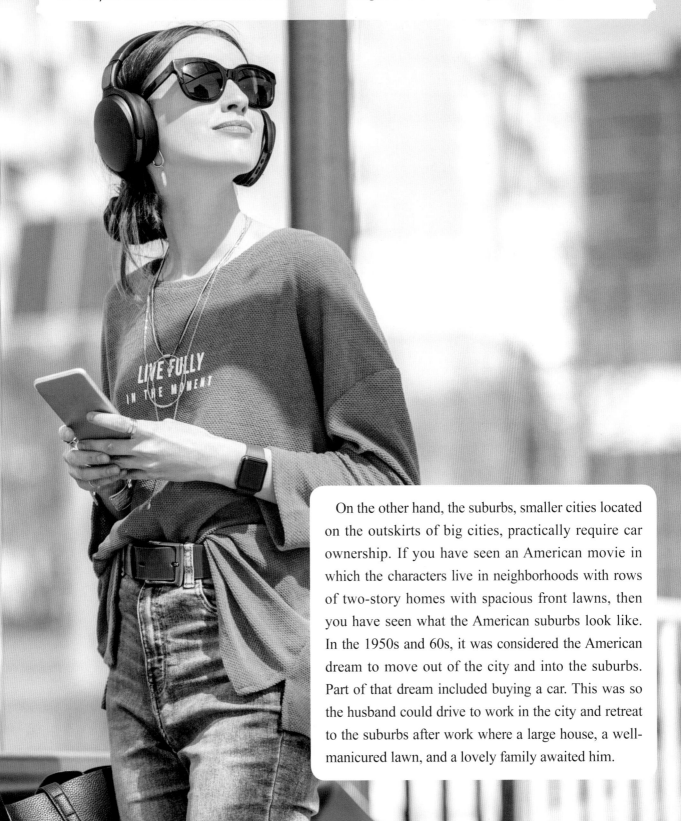

On the other hand, the suburbs, smaller cities located on the outskirts of big cities, practically require car ownership. If you have seen an American movie in which the characters live in neighborhoods with rows of two-story homes with spacious front lawns, then you have seen what the American suburbs look like. In the 1950s and 60s, it was considered the American dream to move out of the city and into the suburbs. Part of that dream included buying a car. This was so the husband could drive to work in the city and retreat to the suburbs after work where a large house, a well-manicured lawn, and a lovely family awaited him.

Conversation 1 *Taking the Bus*

Track 27

A In the United States, it is important to be on time for meetings and other appointments. The same is true for public transportation. Americans hate when a bus or train is not on time. This is a conversation between an American woman, Crystal, and a Ukrainian woman, Mischa. Listen and practice the conversation with a partner.

Crystal and Mischa are waiting for a bus.

Mischa Relax, Crystal. The bus will come when it comes.

Crystal How can you be so calm about it?

Mischa In the Ukraine, the buses are never on time. Sometimes you're lucky, so you only wait five minutes, and sometimes you're not, so you wait 45 minutes.

Crystal But this is Chicago. If the schedule says it will be here at 7:45, it should be here at 7:45. The buses run on time here.

Mischa Is that the bus schedule on your phone?

Crystal Yes, it is.

Mischa Can I look at it for a second?

Crystal Sure.

Mischa You're looking at the wrong schedule. This is the weekday schedule, but today is Saturday.

Crystal You're right. It comes every 30 minutes on the weekend instead of every 15 minutes.

Mischa That's okay. It should be here at 8 o'clock. We only have to wait another 13 minutes.

Crystal Since it only comes twice an hour on weekends, we should take the L train the next time.

⊘ **Words to Know** on time   lucky   schedule

B Practice the conversation with a partner. Use the information in the box below.

A What does the bus schedule say?

B It says bus number 4 comes ¹ _____ .

A So that's ² _____ minutes?

B Yes.

A Then the next bus comes at ³ _____ . We have to wait another ⁴ _____ .

1	2	3	4
three times an hour	every 20	8 o'clock	19 minutes
twice an hour	every 30	6:30	25 minutes
once an hour	every 60	11 o'clock	50

Language Focus

A When riding on the bus or the train in the United States, it is good to know some phrases and expressions which indicate frequency. Look at the chart.

Indicating Frequency		
once an hour	twice a day	three times a week
four times a year	every five minutes	every year

Bus number 1 comes **once an hour**.
My family goes on vacation **twice a year**.
Alice visits her grandmother **three times a week**.
Bus number 33 comes **every five minutes**.
More than 200 flights depart from and arrive at Jeju International Airport **every day**.

B Unscramble the sentences in order to make grammatically correct sentences.

1. church / We / once / go to / a week

2. his car / washes / My father / a month / twice

3. comes / every / Bus number 39 / 10 minutes

4. anniversary party / My parents / every / have / year / a wedding

Speak Out | Pair Work

Find a partner. Then, make sentences by using the expressions above and the bus schedule below. Let your partner guess which bus you are referring to.

Hour	Bus A	Bus B	Bus C	Bus D
7:00	0, 30	0, 12, 24, 36, 48	0, 10, 20, 30, 40, 50	0, 20, 40
8:00	0, 30	0, 12, 24, 36, 48	0, 10, 20, 30, 40, 50	0, 20, 40
9:00	0, 30	0, 12, 24, 36, 48	0, 10, 20, 30, 40, 50	0, 20, 40
10:00	…	…	…	…

A *The bus comes every 30 minutes / twice an hour.*
B *The answer is Bus A.*

Conversation ② *Asking a Bus Driver about a Destination*

Track 28

A America's city bus systems can be difficult to navigate. You may find yourself in a situation where you need to ask a bus driver if the bus you are waiting for actually goes to your destination. This is a conversation between a woman and a bus driver. Listen and practice the conversation with a partner.

Elizabeth is talking to a bus driver.

Elizabeth	Excuse me, sir. Does this bus go to the University of Minnesota?
Bus Driver	It does, but it takes about an hour to get there. There's a more direct route you can take though.
Elizabeth	Could you tell me what that is?
Bus Driver	Sure. Bus number 9 will take you there in about 20 minutes, but it only comes twice an hour, and you just missed it.
Elizabeth	Is there another option?
Bus Driver	There is. If you take bus number 9-1, you will get there in about 30 minutes, and it comes every ten minutes.
Elizabeth	I'll take that one. Thank you so much for your help.
Bus Driver	It's my pleasure, ma'am.

⊘ **Words to Know**   direct   route   option

B Practice the conversation with a partner. Use the information in the box below.

A Excuse me, sir. Does this bus go to ¹ _____ ?

B It does, but bus number ² _____ takes a more direct route.

A Do you know when the next one will come?

B Yes. It comes ³ _____ , so you shouldn't have to wait too long.

A Thank you very much for your help.

B It's my pleasure.

1	2	3
the public library	7	every 15 minutes
the baseball stadium	30-1	three times an hour
the city center	94	every five minutes

Language Focus

A There are several expressions that you can use if you need to ask a bus driver whether or not the bus goes to your destination. Look at the chart.

Does this bus go to ...?	Can I get to ... on this bus?	Will this bus take me to ...?
Does this bus go to the airport? **Does this bus go to** the hotel?	**Can I get to** the hospital **on this bus**? **Can I get to** the library **on this bus**?	**Will this bus take me to** the park? **Will this bus take me to** the museum?

B Complete the conversations by using the correct expressions from the chart. Then, practice the conversations with a partner.

1. A Excuse me, sir. _____ the Grand Hotel?

    B Yes, it will, but bus number 15 will get you there faster. You only have to wait another five minutes.

2. A Excuse me, ma'am. _____ the public library?

    B It does, but there's a more direct route. You should take bus number 2.

3. A I'm sorry to bother you, sir, but _____ the airport _____ ?

    B Yes, you can.

Speak Out | Pair Work

Find a partner. Then, ask your partner questions about the bus routes by using the expressions above.

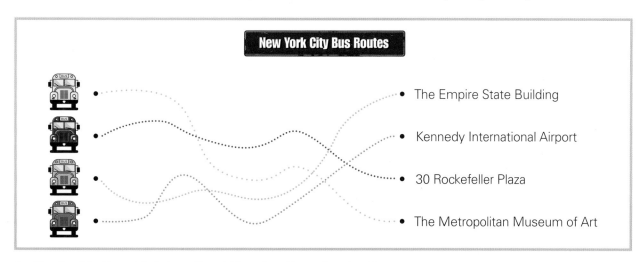

A *Can I get to Kennedy International Airport on the yellow bus?*

B *No, you can't. You can get to the Metropolitan Museum of Art.*

Conversation ③ *Ridesharing Apps*

A The use of ridesharing apps has become very common in the United States. Instead of having to flag down a taxi, you simply notify the app where you are and where you want to go. Then, the nearest driver picks you up and takes you to your destination. You can pay and tip the driver within the app. This is a conversation between a woman and a driver. Listen and practice the conversation with a partner.

Sarah is telling the driver where she would like to be dropped off.

Driver We're getting close to your destination, ma'am.
Would you like me to stop at a specific location?

Sarah Can you drop me off in front of West Coast Steakhouse?

Driver The restaurant is on the other side of the street, ma'am.

Sarah Can you make a U-turn?

Driver I'm sorry, but it's illegal to make a U-turn here. I can take
the second left, go around the block, and come back on the opposite side of the street.
Then, I can drop you off in front of the restaurant.

Sarah No. There's too much traffic. Just drop me off on this side of the street, and I'll use the crosswalk to get to the other side.

Driver Is here okay?

Sarah Yes, right here is fine.

Driver Watch your step, ma'am, and please remember to give me a five-star rating.

Sarah Don't worry. I'll give you a good rating.

⊘ **Words to Know**   drop off   destination   illegal   traffic   crosswalk

B Practice the conversation with a partner. Use the information in the box below.

A Can you drop me off in front of ¹ _____ ?

B The restaurant is on the other side of the road.

A Can you make a U-turn?

B I'm sorry, but it's illegal to make a U-turn here. I can take the second ² _____ , go around the
block, and ³ _____ the opposite side of the street.

1	2	3
BLT Steak	left	come back on
Rising Sun Sushi	right	turn onto
Lobster King	left turn	get onto

Language Focus

A   When using a taxi or ridesharing app, you want to be able to give your driver some specific directions about your destination. Look at some useful expressions for giving directions.

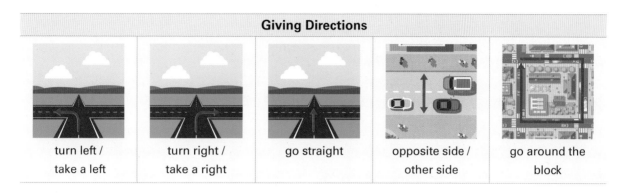

B   Look at the three destinations below. By using the map and the expressions in the chart, explain how you will get to the destinations.

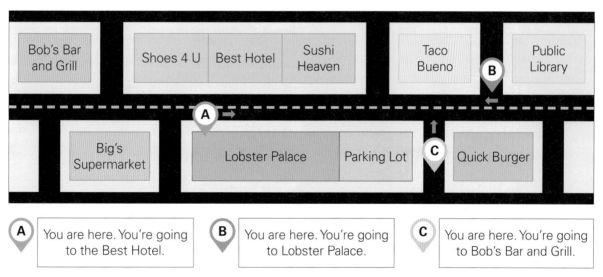

A You are here. You're going to the Best Hotel.	**B** You are here. You're going to Lobster Palace.	**C** You are here. You're going to Bob's Bar and Grill.

I am going to take the second left. Then, I will go around the block, take a right at Sushi Heaven, and go straight to the Best Hotel.

Speak Out | Pair Work

Find a partner. Then, imagine you are a driver and your partner is a passenger in your car. Have your partner give you a starting point and a destination on the map above. Tell your partner how you will get to his or her destination. After that, switch roles.

A   *We are in front of Sushi Heaven, and I want to get to Quick Burger.*

B   *I will take the first left, go around the block, and come back on the opposite side of the street. Then, I will turn right and drop you off in front of Quick Burger.*

Wrap It Up

Fill in the blanks with the correct answers.

1. Hurry up, Janet! I want to be _____ for class.   ⓐ on time   ⓑ lucky

2. The man was fined for _____ parking.   ⓐ direct   ⓑ illegal

3. If we take this bus _____ , we can get there.   ⓐ route   ⓑ destination

4. She will use the _____ to get across the street.   ⓐ traffic   ⓑ crosswalk

5. This route is too long. We need another _____ .   ⓐ option   ⓑ rating

Situation Talk   **Role-play the following situations with a partner.**

Role-Play 1

You are calmly waiting for a bus with a friend.	*You are waiting for a bus with a friend, but you are stressed.*
1. Tell B to relax. Say the bus will come when it comes. 2. Explain that in your country, buses don't run on a regular schedule. Tell B that he or she must be patient. 3. Say okay. 4. Tell B he or she is looking at the weekday schedule, but today is Saturday. The next bus comes at 9:25.	1. Ask A how he or she can be calm. 2. Say okay. Ask A if you can look at the bus schedule on his or her phone. 3. Tell A that it's 9:15 and the bus is ten minutes late. 4. Apologize to A.

Role-Play 2

You are speaking to a bus driver at a bus stop.	*You are a bus driver. You are speaking to a passenger at a bus stop.*
1. Ask B if this bus goes to the baseball stadium. 2. Ask B which bus is faster. 3. Ask B if there's another option. 4. Tell B that you will take that bus. Thank B for his or her help.	1. Tell A that it does go to the baseball stadium, but there is a faster bus. 2. Tell A that the fastest bus is bus number 101, but A just missed it, and it only comes once an hour. 3. Tell A that bus number 302 comes every 20 minutes and only takes 25 minutes to get to the stadium. 4. Tell A that it was no problem.

Too Much Traffic!

🔊 Track 30

Foreigners who come from countries where expansive public transportation systems exist in their cities are often surprised by the lack of public transportation available in the United States, especially in big cities like Los Angeles, where a better public transportation system would be expected. In L.A., foreigners are met with an unruly, gridlocked freeway system which somehow remains insufficient for the amount of traffic it carries.

Unbeknownst to many, before the current Los Angeles freeway system was built, there was a public transportation system consisting of streetcars and buses. However, after World War II, a decision had to be made concerning which direction the city would take. The choices were to expand public transportation or build an elaborate freeway system for automobiles. The latter won.

Now, Los Angeles is stuck with a system which encourages people to drive rather than to use public transportation. Things are starting to change for the better in the city though. Los Angeles has a light rail system that reaches from downtown to the airport. It also has a subway system which stretches from the San Fernando Valley to downtown Los Angeles, giving residents the option to use public transportation.

Cities such as Minneapolis, Minnesota, have built light rail systems which allow people to drive from their homes to large parking lots located just outside the city. These passengers can then take the light rail train from the parking lots to the downtown area where their workplaces are located. These kinds of solutions are being implemented in more and more cities in the USA as people get sick and tired of spending inordinate amounts of time sitting in traffic.

Read the article. Answer these questions.
1. What are the problems with Los Angeles's freeway system?
2. What kind of public transportation system did Los Angeles have before World War II?
3. What have cities like Minneapolis done to combat the lack of parking in the downtown areas?

Entertainment

🅑 Track 31

Common Types of Entertainment in the USA

Many popular forms of entertainment in the United States revolve around the consumption of alcohol. There are, however, some more wholesome activities that Americans also like to engage in. Going to the movies is still one of the most popular forms of entertainment in the USA. Unfortunately, the cost of movie tickets over the past ten to fifteen years has increased rather dramatically. Despite the increased ticket prices, Americans still love to see films on the big screen. The enormous budgets for blockbuster films like the Marvel Comics films help filmmakers create on-screen spectacles for moviegoers.

Americans also enjoy going to live concerts. Tickets for the most popular artists performing at the largest venues in big cities can often be purchased through a company named Ticketmaster. This is usually done online and with a credit card. On the day of the show,

you drive to the venue and park in the large parking lot near the site. Venues are usually sports stadiums or coliseums. Do not forget to bring some extra money for parking as it is not included in the ticket price.

For the most financially responsible Americans, parks are great places to enjoy the city without spending too much money. Cycling and in-line skating are possible for those looking to get some exercise and reduce stress. And bigger parks often have concession stands where beverages and snacks can be purchased. There may even be restaurants, cafes, and rental shops where bicycles can be rented by the hour.

Discuss the following questions.

1. How often do you go to the movies in your country?
2. Do you enjoy going to live concerts in your country? When was the last time you went to a concert?
3. What can you do at parks in your country? Do vendors sell food at parks? Can you rent bicycles by the hour?

Conversation ① *Buying Movie Tickets*

Track 32

A If you are seventeen years old or older, it is a good idea to bring picture ID to the movie theater in case you want to see an R-rated movie. There is a chance that the clerk will ask to see your ID, so it is better to be safe than sorry. This is a conversation between a woman and a clerk at the box office. Listen and practice the conversation with a partner.

Janine is buying movie tickets at the ticket booth.

Clerk   Can I help you?

Janine   Yes. I'd like two tickets for *My Summer Romance*.

Clerk   Which showing would you like tickets for?

Janine   The 9:15.

Clerk   I'm sorry, but the 9:15 is sold out.

Janine   When's the next showing?

Clerk   We have some available seats for the 9:55 showing.

Janine   Okay, that's fine.

Clerk   This movie is rated R, so I need to see your IDs to make sure you are both seventeen years old or older.

Janine   No problem. Here's my driver's license, and here's my friend's driver's license.

Clerk   These look fine. So that's two adults for the 9:55?

Janine   That's correct.

Clerk   Here are your tickets. Enjoy the show!

⊘ **Words to Know**   showing   sold out   available   driver's license

---

B Practice the conversation with a partner. Use the information in the box below.

A   I'd like two tickets for the 9:15 showing of ¹ _____ .

B   Sorry, but the 9:15 is sold out. We have some available seats for the ² _____ showing.

A   Okay, that's fine.

B   This movie is rated R, so I'm going to have to check your IDs to make sure you are both seventeen years old or older.

A   No problem. Here's my ³ _____ , and here's my friend's driver's license.

1	2	3
Fatal Descent	10:05	student ID
Unreasonable Doubt	9:35	passport
Planetary Justice	9:50	green card

Language Focus

A Americans tend to carry at least one valid form of picture identification (ID card) with them at all times because they never know when they might be asked to show it. Here are some common expressions Americans use when asking to see ID and some common forms of ID.

Asking for Identification	Common Forms of Identification	
May/Can I see your ID? Please show me your ID. I need to see your driver's license. I need to check your passport.	• driver's license • student ID card • birth certificate • green card (permanent resident card)	• passport • military ID

B Complete the conversation by writing the appropriate forms of ID in the blanks.

A How can I help you?

B I'd like one ticket for *Hell House*, please.

A You must be at least 17 years old to see this movie. Can I see your _____ ?

B I'm sorry, but I don't drive.

A Can I check your _____ ?

B I don't have one of those either because I've never traveled overseas. My wife is an American citizen, so I have a _____ . It has my picture and my date of birth on it.

A That will work.

Speak Out | Pair Work

Find a partner. Then, take turns buying tickets to the movies on the schedule.

Movie Schedule				
The Soldier	(PG)	4:00	5:30	7:45
Hell House	(R)	5:55	6:55	9:00
Zoo Friends	(G)	6:00	8:00	8:30
Black Ice	(PG-13)	5:25	6:50	9:30
Cupid's Eros	(NC-17)	7:00	9:15	11:00

*Movie Rating System in the USA

G:	general audiences
PG:	parental guidance suggested
PG-13:	parents strongly cautioned; may be inappropriate for children under 13
R:	restricted; under 17 requires a parent or accompanying adult
NC-17:	no one 17 or under admitted

A *I'd like one ticket for* Cupid's Eros, *please.*

B *Which showing would you like a ticket for?*

A *The eleven o'clock showing.*

B *I need to see your ID. You must be 18 years old to see this movie.*

A *Here you are.*

⊚Track 33

A Concert tickets for very popular acts in the United States can be very difficult to acquire. Oftentimes, tickets sell out very quickly online. Are tickets for popular groups and artists difficult to acquire in your country? Listen and practice the conversation with a partner.

Tyler and Cindy are having a telephone conversation.

Cindy Hello?

Tyler I got the tickets!

Cindy To the Katy Perry concert?

Tyler That's right.

Cindy No way!

Tyler Guess where we're sitting.

Cindy Where?

Tyler Ten rows from the front.

Cindy Are you kidding me? How did you get them?

Tyler At twenty to nine, I logged in to the ticketing website. At nine o'clock on the nose, I hit the purchase button. Thirty seconds later, the transaction went through.

Cindy We're so lucky.

Tyler I know. It's only ten past nine now, and tickets are already sold out.

⊘ **Words to Know**   row   on the nose   transaction

B Practice the conversation with a partner. Use the information in the box below.

A I got the tickets for ¹ _____ !

B No way! How did you get them?

A At ² _____ twelve, I logged in to the ticketing website. At twelve o'clock ³ _____ , I hit the purchase button. A minute later, the transaction went through.

B We are so lucky.

A I know. It's only ⁴ _____ twelve now, and tickets are already sold out.

1	2	3	4
the Taylor Swift concert	a quarter to	on the dot	five past
Hamilton, the musical	twenty-five to	on the button	a quarter past
the World Cup finals	five to	on the nose	ten after

Language Focus

A Americans use a number of different time expressions in their daily lives. Here are the most popular time expressions in English that peolpe visiting the country should know.

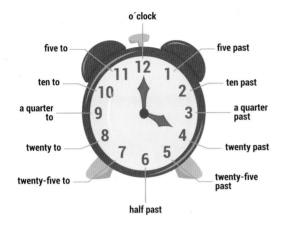

Telling Time	
11:00	It's eleven o'clock.
2:10	It's ten past two.
7:15	It's a quarter past seven.
12:30	It's half past twelve.
9:35	It's twenty-five to ten.
5:45	It's a quarter to six.
3:55	It's five to four.

B Write the correct times by using the time expressions above.

1.

2.

3.

4.

Speak Out | Pair Work

Write times by using intervals of five minutes. Then, write some activities in the table. Invite your partner to do the activities. When your partner asks you what time they start, tell him or her the times by using the time expressions above.

6:30	go to a Taylor Swift concert

A *Would you like to go to a Taylor Swift concert?*

B *Sure. What time does it start?*

A *It starts at half past six. We should be at the stadium at a quarter past six.*

🔊 Track 34

A America is a large country with a lot of land. Because of this, there are a lot of public parks available for those living there. Many parks contain bike paths, basketball courts, and tennis courts. Public parks are free to use; however, you must bring your own basketball, tennis racket, and tennis balls. Listen and practice the conversation with a partner.

Michael and Nicki are riding their bikes at the park.

Michael Look at that sunset, Nic. Isn't it beautiful?

Nicki It sure is.

Michael Do you want to go around the park one more time?

Nicki What time is it?

Michael A quarter to seven. When do we have to return the bikes?

Nicki We rented them at ten after six, so we have them for another twenty-five minutes.

Michael Is that enough time to go around the entire park?

Nicki Not the entire park, but I know a shorter route. It only takes twenty minutes.

Michael Okay, let's do it. And when we're done, I'll buy you some ice cream.

Nicki Oh, I love the ice cream here. Have you tried the pistachio?

Michael Not yet. I'm more of a chocolate chip person.

Nicki You've got to try the pistachio. It's to die for!

Michael Okay, you've convinced me. I'm going to try it.

✅ Words to Know   sunset   rent   entire   convince

B Practice the conversation with a partner. Use the information in the box below.

A ¹ _____ get some ice cream at the Ice Cream Shack?

B Oh, I love the ice cream there. Have you tried the pistachio?

A Not yet. I'm more of a ² _____ person.

B ³ _____ try the pistachio. It's to die for!

A Okay, you've convinced me. I'm going to try it.

1	2	3
Would you like to	vanilla	You have got to
Are you in the mood to	Neapolitan	You need to
Should we	cookies 'n' cream	I'm begging you to

Language Focus

A Americans often blend certain words together to form what sounds like one word. Here are some examples of common reductions used in American English. Remember that reductions are not actually words and should only be used when speaking, not when writing.

Blended Words (Reductions)		
want to → *wanna*	got to → *gotta*	going to → *gonna*
would you → *woudja*	should have → *shouda/shouduv*	

B Read the sentences aloud by using reductions.

1. Do you want to ride bikes around the park?

2. We've got to get some ice cream after the game.

3. Yuck! I don't like pistachio ice cream. I should have bought cookies 'n' cream.

4. We're going to go to the park on Sunday.

5. Would you like to go to the BTS concert next Friday?

6. You should have been ready by now. Now, we are going to be late!

7. I've got to get tickets to the Red Velvet concert. I want to see them so bad*!

* Americans sometimes delete the "ly" from adverbs in conversational English. ex. badly → bad

Speak Out | Pair Work

Complete the dialogue with your choice of information. Then, practice your dialogue with a partner. Use reductions when you see the underlined phrases.

A Do you want to _____ (activity) tonight?

B Sure. What time should I be ready?

A I think we should be there at _____ (time).

B I've got to take a shower and get ready. Can we make it a quarter after?

A That's fine. Would you like me to pick you up?

B Sure. I'm going to ask my roommate, _____ (roommate's name), if he/she wants to come. Is that okay?

A Of course. The more the merrier!

Wrap It Up

Complete the sentences by using the words in the box.

sold out	on the nose	entire	sunset	convinced

1. I can't believe you ate the _____ ice cream cone by yourself. You didn't save me a bite!

2. Jongmin finally _____ his girlfriend to try bubble tea, and she liked it.

3. Oh, look at the horizon. Isn't the _____ beautiful?

4. Let's meet at twelve o'clock _____.

5. I'm sorry, sir. There aren't any more tickets. They are _____.

Situation Talk

A **Role-play the following situation with a partner.**

Role **A**	Role **B**
You are a clerk at a movie theater.	*You are buying movie tickets at a movie theater.*
1. Ask B how you can help him or her.	1. Say you want to buy two tickets to *My Boyfriend, the Zombie.*
2. Ask B which showing you want tickets for.	2. Say you want tickets for the 10:10 showing.
3. Tell B that you are sorry, but the 10:10 showing is sold out.	3. Ask A when the next showing is.
4. Say the next showing is at 10:55.	4. Tell A that you would like two tickets for the 10:55 showing.
5. Ask B for identification.	5. Show your green card and your friend's driver's license.

B **Find a partner. Then, make sentences about the pictures by using reductions.**

A *Would you like to play tennis at the park? / I'm going to play tennis at the park. Will you join me?*
B *Yes. I definitely want to do that!*

Different Hobbies in Different Places

Track 35

The United States is a large country geographically and contains numerous regions with different climates. In the northern states of the Midwest and New England, winters tend to be extremely cold with lots of snowfall. In the Pacific Northwest, states like Washington and Oregon have milder winters with less snowfall and more rainfall. The land is lush and full of green foliage. In the Southwestern United States, places such as Arizona and New Mexico have large desert regions where temperatures in the winter are mild but get dangerously hot in the summer. People in these places tend to spend more time in air-conditioned malls and movie theaters in the summer than outside in the burning hot sun.

Given the diversity of the climate and terrain in the U.S., it is not illogical to think that the hobbies people pursue in these regions are a little different. For example, if you grew up in the state of Colorado, there is a very good chance you have spent some time skiing or snowboarding in the Rocky Mountains. If you grew up in Miami, going to the beach and swimming were probably things you and all of your friends enjoyed. In the Midwest and New England, hockey is a popular sport while in Texas, American football and baseball are far more popular. Golf is one of those hobbies that people everywhere are crazy about, but it can only be played in the spring, summer, and fall in some states while it can be played all year round in warmer states. If you are planning on living in the United States, it would be worth your time to do a little research about the climate and terrain. Find out what kinds of activities people do in those places. Perhaps you will find a new hobby and make some new friends in the process.

Read the article. Check T for true or F for false.
1. The USA contains multiple regions with similar climates.   T ☐ / F ☐
2. States in the Southwestern USA get dangerously hot in the summer. T ☐ / F ☐
3. Golf is popular in many regions in the United States.   T ☐ / F ☐

Unit 08

More than Just Great Coffee

Premium Coffee in America

Coffee is a beverage that has been around in the United States for centuries. Although it feels as though they have been around forever, too, premium coffee chains such as Starbucks, Caribou Coffee, and the Coffee Bean & Tea Leaf have only been around for the past 30 years or so. In the 1980s, Starbucks founder, and former CEO, Howard Schultz visited Milan, Italy and realized that nothing like the Italian cafés there existed in America. The cafés in Italy had cheerful atmospheres and provided common spaces that residents in the neighborhoods could enjoy.

1. How many cups of coffee or tea do you usually drink in a day?
2. How often do you visit coffee shops in your country?
3. If you enjoy visiting coffee shops in your country, who do you usually go with?

Schultz wanted to bring the Italian-style café back to the United States. At that time, Americans were more likely to drink coffee at a local diner than at a café. When Schultz brought the Italian-style café to America in the form of Starbucks, its popularity soared. Imitators sprang up everywhere, and a new form of coffee culture was born in the United States. Employees at Starbucks learned to become skilled baristas and developed a deep understanding of coffee, similar to the Italian baristas Schultz had met in Milan. Premium coffee chains like Starbucks have become a global trend over the past 30 years.

Conversation 1 Ordering a Cup of Coffee

Track 37

A Americans often make special requests when ordering coffee at coffee shops. This is a conversation between a customer and a clerk at a coffee shop. Listen and practice the conversation with a partner.

Zach is purchasing a cup of coffee at a premium coffee chain.

Clerk   How can I help you?

Zach   I'd like a cappuccino and a brownie.

Clerk   How do you take your cappuccino?

Zach   With a dash of cinnamon. And can I get a sprinkle of powdered sugar on the brownie?

Clerk   No problem. Will that be all for you today?

Zach   I'll take a sparkling water, too.

Clerk   Okay, so that's one cappuccino with a dash of cinnamon, a brownie with a sprinkle of powdered sugar, and a sparkling water?

Zach   Yes, that's right.

Clerk   That'll be $17.83.

Zach   Here's $20.

Clerk   And here's your change.

Zach   That's okay. Put it in the tip jar.

Clerk   Thank you, sir.

⊘ Words to Know   take   dash   sprinkle   change   tip jar

B Practice the conversation with a partner. Use the information in the box below.

A   How can I help you?

B   I'd like a ¹_____ and a ²_____.

A   How do you take your ¹_____?

B   With a ³_____ of cinnamon. And can I get a sprinkle of powdered sugar on the ²_____?

A   No problem.

1	2	3
bubble tea	piece of chocolate cake	pinch
soy latte	glazed donut	dash
latte macchiato	croissant	sprinkle

Language Focus

A There are a number of expressions that American English speakers use to describe adding spices and flavoring to foods and beverages. Here are some of the most common expressions.

Liquids	Powders	
a splash of ...	a pinch of ...	a dash of ...
a drop of ... / a few drops of ...	a sprinkle of ...	a packet of ...
I'd like **a splash of** milk in my coffee. I'd like **a splash of** lemon in my water. Can I get **a few drops of** syrup in my latte? Could I get **a drop of** honey in my tea?	I'd like **a pinch of** cinnamon in my Americano. Could I get **a dash of** nutmeg in my latte? Can I get **a sprinkle of** sugar on my muffin? I'd love **a packet of** sugar in my coffee.	

B Look at the pictures and write what is added to the foods and drinks by using the expressions in the chart.

He is adding _____ .

1. _____
2. _____
3. _____
4. _____
5. _____
6. _____

Speak Out | Pair Work

Take turns ordering a coffee and a dessert from a partner. Tell your partner how you take your coffee and dessert.

Coffee		Desserts	
Espresso	2.00	Chocolate Muffin	3.50
Americano	3.00	Oatmeal Cookie	2.00
Café Latte	3.50	Cheesecake	5.50
Cappuccino	3.50	Chocolate Brownie	5.00

A *How can I help you?*

B *I'd like an Americano and a chocolate muffin.*

A *How do you take your ...?*

Conversation ② *A First Date at a Coffee Shop*

A Coffee shops are popular places for first dates. If the date goes well, the couple can decide to have dinner or see a movie, but if it does not go well, they can finish their drinks and go their own separate ways. This is a conversation between a man and a woman who are on a first date at a coffee shop. Listen and practice the conversation with a partner.

Greg and Carla are having their first date at a coffee shop.

Greg Carla, over here!

Carla Hi, Greg.

Greg Did you find the coffee shop all right?

Carla Yes. Your directions were great.

Greg I was worried that you might have gotten lost.

Carla I'm so sorry I'm late. My mother called me just as I was leaving my apartment.

Greg That's okay. I've only been waiting for a few minutes.

Carla This coffee shop is really cute.

Greg It's my favorite. The chocolate muffins here are made from scratch. They're delicious. Would you like to try one?

Carla Maybe later. Right now, I'm really craving a double espresso soy latte.

Greg I'm dying for a caramel macchiato. How do you take your latte?

Carla Just a pinch of cinnamon and one packet of Splenda.

Greg Okay. I'll be right back with our drinks.

✓ **Words to Know** directions from scratch crave

B Practice the conversation with a partner. Use the information in the box below.

A Did you find the ¹ _____ all right?

B Yes. Your directions were ² _____ .

A I was worried that you might have gotten lost.

B I'm sorry I'm late. ³ _____ just as I was leaving my apartment.

1	2	3
coffee shop	excellent	My sister called me
café	spot on	My dog needed to go outside
bistro	perfect	My landlord wanted to check the fire alarms

Language Focus

A We often find ourselves in situations where we need to apologize for being late or missing a phone call or appointment. Here are some common expressions for apologizing as well as some reasons. Look at the chart.

Apologizing	Giving Reasons/Excuses
I'm sorry I'm late for our date.	My mother called me just as I was leaving the house.
I'm really sorry I missed your phone call.	I was in the shower when you called.
I'm truly sorry I forgot your birthday.	There's no excuse for it.
I apologize for missing your speech.	I overslept this morning.

B Complete the apologies by using the expressions from the chart.

1. _____ I missed your phone call.

2. _____ I am late for class.

3. _____ missing your performance.

4. _____ I'm late for our date.

5. _____ I forgot our wedding anniversary.

6. _____ missing your dinner party.

Speak Out | Pair Work

Read the apologies above to a partner. Then, look at the pictures and say why you are apologizing.

A *I'm sorry I missed your phone call. I dropped my phone, and now it's broken.*
B *Don't worry about it.*

Conversation ③ *Coming Over for a Cup of Coffee*

A It is very common in America to invite a friend over for a cup of coffee or tea. This is a conversation between a guest and a host having coffee together. Listen and practice the conversation with a partner.

Haerin is having a cup of coffee at Lucy's apartment.

Lucy (*doorbell rings*) Who is it?

Haerin It's Haerin.

Lucy Hey, come on in. It's great to see you!

Haerin It's great to see you, too!

Lucy I just put a pot of coffee on. Can I pour you a cup?

Haerin Is it decaf?

Lucy No, it's regular.

Haerin I've been watching my caffeine intake lately, but it's only 10:00 a.m., so one cup isn't going to kill me.

Lucy It's really good. I joined an online coffee club about six months ago. Each month, I get a different flavor.

Haerin What's this month's flavor?

Lucy This month, I received a light Colombian roast. It tastes really good, and it isn't too strong.

Haerin That sounds amazing.

Lucy How do you take it?

Haerin Black is fine.

✔ **Words to Know** decaf intake flavor roast

B Practice the conversation with a partner. Use the information in the box below.

A I joined ¹ .... club about six months ago. Each month, I get a different flavor.

B What's this month's ² .... ?

A It's ³ .... They're really good.

B That sounds amazing.

1	2	3
a steak of the month	meat	a package of T-bone steaks
a cookie	cookies	a box of macaroon cookies
an apple	apples	a crate of Golden Delicious apples

Language Focus

A   **Here are some common expressions for containers. Look at the chart.**

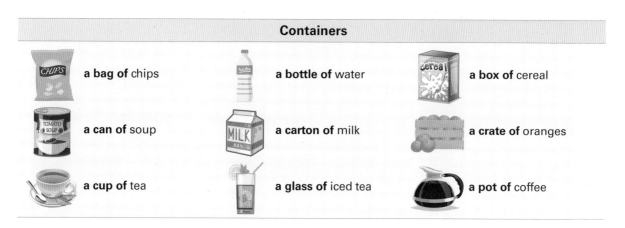

Containers		
a bag of chips	**a bottle of** water	**a box of** cereal
a can of soup	**a carton of** milk	**a crate of** oranges
a cup of tea	**a glass of** iced tea	**a pot of** coffee

B   **Look at the pictures. Then, write the correct food items and containers.**

1.

2.

3.

4.

5.

6.

7.

8.

Speak Out | Pair Work

Write some food items you need to buy by using the expressions for containers above. Then, take turns ordering the items from your partner.

Shopping List

- [ ] *two bags of rice*
- [ ]
- [ ]
- [ ]
- [ ]

A *Can I get some rice? / I'd like to order ...*
B *Of course. How much rice would you like?*
A *I'd like two bags of rice.*

Wrap It Up

Match the words with their correct definitions.

1. intake   •

2. tip jar   •

3. from scratch •

4. crave   •

5. flavor   •

• ⓐ homemade; not store bought

• ⓑ a container in which people can put tips for good service in

• ⓒ to want something very much

• ⓓ the taste of something

• ⓔ the kinds of foods, nutrients, and chemicals you decide to put into your body

Situation Talk

A **Find a partner. Then, create a coffee shop by coming up with a name for the coffee shop and a menu with coffee drinks and desserts. Include the prices for your drinks and desserts. Finally, take turns ordering coffee and dessert from one another. Make sure to ask your customer how he or she takes his or her drinks and desserts.**

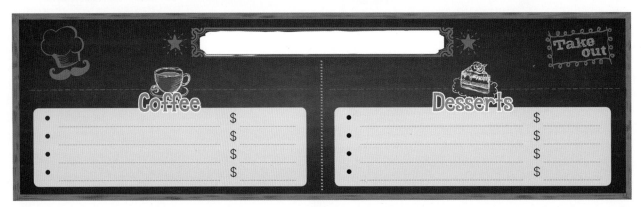

B **Role-play the following situation with a partner.**

You are meeting B for a date at a coffee shop.	*You are meeting A for a date at a coffee shop.*
1. Say hello to B.	1. Tell A that you are sorry you are late.
2. Tell B that you have only been waiting for ten minutes.	2. Give A the reason why you are late.
3. Say "That's okay." Ask B what he or she would like to drink.	3. Tell A that you would like a soy latte.
4. Ask B how he or she takes his or her soy latte.	4. Say that you would like a pinch of nutmeg and a packet of Splenda in it.
5. Say that you will be right back with the drinks.	

Coffee Today vs. Coffee in the Past

Track 40

The way Americans think about coffee these days is different than how they thought about it in the past. In the 1970s and 1980s, coffee was not considered a profitable drink for many restaurants in the United States. In fact, a lot of diners in America offered customers a bottomless pot of coffee, meaning they could have as many refills as they wanted for the price of one cup. This also included small cups of cream and sugar packets, which were placed on every table in the diner.

Premium coffee shops like Starbucks changed coffee in a profound way. They provided customers with a nicely decorated interior, a warm atmosphere, and comfortable seating in which customers could enjoy their beverages. They also increased the menu options by creating recipes for a variety of caffeinated and non-caffeinated drinks and by giving customers the option to buy tasty baked goods to go along with their drinks.

Starbucks and its counterparts were able to charge high prices for their drinks because the spaces they had created attracted so many customers. By the mid-90s, coffee was no longer considered a cheap beverage. In fact, premium coffee shops turned coffee into a luxury item. Everyone wanted to be seen walking down the street with Starbucks logos on their cups. Premium coffee chains wanted their customers to feel sophisticated and proud that they were drinking good coffee, not coffee made from coffee crystals that came from a plastic container. In the past 30 years, coffee's image has changed dramatically in the USA due to the influence of Starbucks and other premium coffee chains, a trend which now spans the entire globe.

Read the article. Answer these questions.
1. What does "a bottomless pot of coffee" mean?
2. Which company changed the way Americans think about coffee?
3. How do premium coffee chains want their customers to feel?

Bars and Nightclubs

⊙Track 41

Popular Places to Drink in America

Besides going to coffee shops, bars are probably the most popular places for friends to sit and chat, for boyfriends and girlfriends to enjoy each other's company, and for coworkers to unwind after a hard day at work. Although bars can be busy during the weekdays, the weekends are when they receive the largest number of customers. This is also true for nightclubs. Whereas you might dress more casually for a night out at a bar, those heading out to a nightclub always dress to the nines. Nightclubs are noisier than bars, too. So if you want to spend the night having polite conversation, a nightclub is not the best location for doing that. A bar is a much better choice.

There are many different types of bars, too. New, trendy bars in big cities attract a younger, classier clientele. Drink prices at these places are usually much more expensive. Sports bars, which can be found anywhere in the United States, attract customers both young and old and offer reasonably priced drinks, greasy food, and big screens where important sports games can be watched. Like bars, dance clubs attract all kinds of people, although young people are more likely to spend an evening at a nightclub than a person over 40. Each dance club caters to people who enjoy different genres of music, such as electronic dance music, salsa music, and rock 'n' roll music.

Conversation **1** *Trying to Get into the Bar*

◉Track **42**

A In the United States, you must be 21 years old in order to purchase and consume alcohol. In fact, it is a rite of passage for many young men and women to enter a bar at 12:00 a.m. on the day of their 21st birthday by using their official driver's license. This is a conversation between a woman and a security guard at a bar. Listen and practice the conversation with a partner.

Minhee is trying to enter a bar so that she can drink alcohol with her friends.

Security Can I see your driver's license, please?

Minhee It's okay. I'm 21.

Security That may be true, but I'm still going to need to see your ID if you want to drink here.

Minhee But I don't have a driver's license. I don't drive.

Security Do you have another form of identification?

Minhee I have a credit card.

Security Sorry, but it has to be a picture ID with your date of birth on it.

Minhee Will you accept a passport?

Security Of course.

Minhee Here's my passport.

Security It says here you were born August 21, 2000. You must be 21 years old to legally drink in this state. Sorry.

Minhee In my country, the drinking age is nineteen years old.

Security We're not in your country, are we?

⊘ **Words to Know**   ID(identification)   date of birth   legally

---

B Practice the conversation with a partner. Use the information in the box below.

A I need to check a picture ID with your date of birth on it.

B Will you accept a ¹ _____ ?

A Of course.

B Here it is.

A It says here you were born ² _____ . You must be 21 years old to ³ _____ in this state.

1	2	3
driver's license	January 25, 2000	drink alcohol
passport	February 11, 2001	purchase cigarettes
student ID	July 5, 2000	gamble

Language Focus

A When showing identification, it might be necessary to give your date of birth on your ID. Security at nightclubs and bars often test fake ID holders by asking them their DOBs. If the cardholders cannot "remember" their own birthdays, security knows the people are carrying fake IDs. Learn how to read dates in English.

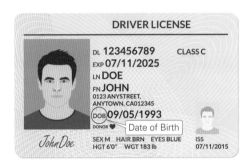

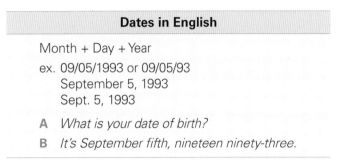

Dates in English

Month + Day + Year

ex. 09/05/1993 or 09/05/93
September 5, 1993
Sept. 5, 1993

A *What is your date of birth?*

B *It's September fifth, nineteen ninety-three.*

B Say the birthdates aloud.

1. DOB 01/25/1977
2. DOB 09/04/2008
3. DOB 11/11/1999
4. DOB 05/15/2002
5. DOB 08/30/2004

Speak Out | Pair Work

Find a partner. Then, try to purchase the items or participate in the activities below by using your own driver's license or another form of picture identification with your DOB on it. If you do not meet the minimum age requirement, your partner should deny your attempt.

| 21 years old | 21 years old | 18 years old | 18 years old | 21 years old |

A *I'd like to buy these cigarettes.*

B *I need to see your ID. What is your date of birth?*

A *It's January 18, 1998.*

Conversation ② *At the Bar*

Track 43

A In a bar in the United States, you can pay for each drink individually, or you can open a tab. When you open a tab, you have to leave your credit card with your bartender or server. The bartender or server keeps track of the drinks that you order on your tab and then has you pay the total at the end of the night. This is a conversation between a man and a server at a bar. Listen and practice the conversation with a partner.

Chen is drinking with three other friends at a bar.

Chen   Can I open a tab?

Server   Do you have a credit card?

Chen   I sure do. Is my VISA card okay?

Server   No problem. What can I get for you?

Chen   I think we'll start with a round of beers. Do you have Miller Lite on tap?

Server   We sure do. I'll be right back with your drinks.

(at the end of the evening)

Server   Here's your tab.

Chen   Thank you.

Server   You're welcome.

Chen   Hey, everyone. Our tab comes to $79.97. If the four of us pay $25.00 each, that would amount to a 20% tip. What do you think?

Chen's Friends   *(together)* It sounds good to me. Me, too. Cool.

Chen   So I'll take care of the tab, and you guys give me $25.00 each.

⊘ **Words to Know**   tab   a round of   on tap

B Practice the conversation with a partner. Use the information in the box below.

A Can I open a tab?

B Do you have a credit card?

A Is my ¹_____ okay?

B No problem. What ²_____ ?

A I think we'll start with a round of ³_____ .

1	2	3
VISA card	can I get for you	beers
MasterCard	would you like to drink	shots
American Express card	would you like to order	cocktails

Language Focus

A In America, it is especially common to split the tab with a group of friends at the bar. Here are some common expressions Americans use in regard to tabs.

Opening a Tab	Keeping the Tab Open / Closing the Tab	Buying Someone a Drink
Can I open a tab?	I'd like to keep the tab open.	Put it on my tab.
I'd like to open a tab.	I'd like to close the tab.	You can put it on my tab.
I want to open a tab.	I want to close the tab.	

B Complete the dialogues by using the expressions in the chart. Then, read them aloud.

1. Customer _____

    Server   Okay. Do you have a credit card?

    Customer Do you take MasterCard?

    Server   Of course.

    (at the end of the evening)

    Server   Your group is getting smaller. Would you like to close the tab?

    Customer Yes. _____

2. Server   Your group is shrinking. Would you like to close the tab?

    Customer No. _____

                Do you see the woman in the red shirt ordering a beer?

    Server   Yes.

    Customer _____

    Server   No problem. I'll put it on your tab.

Speak Out | Pair Work

Find a partner. Then, read about two experiences at bars. After that, decide how much each person should contribute to the tab in each situation.

Nate's Bar & Grill	O'Reilly's Pub
Service: Excellent	**Service**: Terrible
Tab Total: $249.99	**Tab Total**: $200.05
Number of Friends: 4	**Number of Friends**: 5
Cardholder: You	**Cardholder**: You
Each Person's Total: $	**Each Person's Total**: $

A *How much should we tip the server?*

B *I think 25% is good.*

A *Okay.*

B *Each person owes me $62, but I'll take $60.*

Conversation ③ Designated Drivers

A Americans often have to drive to bars and nightclubs. If you are going out with friends, make sure one of your friends is the designated driver for the night. The designated driver is the person who remains sober all night, so he or she can drive his or her friends to the bar or club and safely home again. Listen and practice the conversation with a partner.

Claire is the designated driver, but she is drinking and dancing at the club.

Claire   I love this club, Anthony! Tonight's ladies' night, so I can drink for free all night long. Ooh, they're playing my favorite song. Come and dance with me!

Anthony   Wait. I'm just worried because you drove us here tonight. You're the designated driver.

Claire   Oh, don't worry. I've only had a couple of drinks. Anyway, I drive better when I'm a little tipsy.

Anthony   You've had more than a couple. That's your third glass of champagne.

Claire   Chill out, Anthony. Don't be such a downer.

Anthony   I'm just looking out for you and our friends.

Claire   No, you're not. You're ruining my buzz.

Anthony   Look. I haven't had anything to drink yet. Why don't you give me your car keys, and I'll drive everyone home? And tomorrow morning, I'll drop your car off at your apartment.

Claire   Are you going to dance with me if I give you my keys?

Anthony   I promise.

⊘ **Words to Know**   designated   tipsy   chill out   downer   buzz

B Practice the conversation with a partner. Use the information in the box below.

A   You're ¹ _____ .

B   Look. I haven't had anything to drink yet. Why don't you give me your car keys, and I'll drive you home? And tomorrow morning, I'll ² _____ your car to your apartment.

A   Are you going to dance with me if I give you my keys?

B   ³ _____ !

1	2	3
bringing me down	bring	For sure
bumming me out	take	Absolutely
killing my buzz	drive	You got it

Language Focus

A When drinking at bars or nightclubs, you may find yourself having to negotiate with a drunk person. This can be especially difficult if the other person is extremely intoxicated. One of the ways we negotiate in English is by using the first conditional. Look at the chart.

The First Conditional	
Condition	Result
If you give me your keys,	I will drive you home.
If you don't leave with me now,	I won't buy you any fast food.
If you ask me nicely,	I will help you study.
Result	Condition
I will be the designated driver next week	if you are the designated driver tonight.
We can wake up early and play basketball	if we don't go to the club tonight.
I won't return your sunglasses	if you don't return my blue jeans.

B Complete the sentences by using the given information.

1. `Condition` you pay for dinner   `Result` I pay for the movie

   I'll pay for the movie if you pay for dinner. / If you pay for dinner, I'll pay for the movie.

2. `Condition` you wake up early in the morning   `Result` I go jogging with you

3. `Condition` you tell the truth   `Result` I'm not angry

4. `Condition` you lend me your car this weekend   `Result` I buy you a drink next weekend

Speak Out

Imagine your friend is the designated driver, but he has decided to start drinking at the bar anyway. Negotiate with him by offering him three solutions to the problem by using the first conditional.

If you don't drink tonight, I'll _____ .

If _____ .

_____ .

I'm not even a little drunk!

Wrap It Up

Vocabulary Check — Fill in the blanks with the correct answers.

1. I need to see some form of picture _____ .   ⓐ date of birth   ⓑ ID

2. Excuse me. Do you have Guinness beer _____ ?   ⓐ on tap   ⓑ tab

3. You can't _____ drink in this country until you are 21.   ⓐ designated   ⓑ legally

4. _____ , Dave! You're so uptight. You need to relax.   ⓐ Chill out   ⓑ Buzz

5. I don't think Elliot should drive. He's a little _____ .   ⓐ tipsy   ⓑ downer

Situation Talk

A   **Role-play the following situations with a partner.**

Role-Play 1

Role **A**	Role **B**
You are security at a bar entrance.	*You are trying to enter a bar.*
1. Ask B for his or her driver's license. 2. Ask B if he or she has a different form of ID. 3. Tell B that it has to be a picture ID. 4. Tell B that a passport is fine. Ask B for his or her date of birth.	1. Tell A that you do not have a driver's license. 2. Tell A that you have a credit card. 3. Ask A if a passport would be acceptable. 4. Say your birthdate.

Role-Play 2

Role **A**	Role **B**
You are paying the tab at a bar with your credit card.	*You are splitting the tab with your friend.*
1. Tell B that the tab is $85.94. 2. Tell B that you thought the service was good. Suggest 20%. 3. Tell B that if he or she gives you $50, you will call it even.	1. Ask A how much he or she thinks the two of you should tip. 2. Agree with A on a 20% tip. Tell A that that comes to approximately $103. 3. Agree to give A $50.

B   **Complete the first conditional sentences. Compare your answers with a partner's answers.**

1. If you are the designated driver this weekend, _____ .

2. I will drive you to school this week _____ .

3. If you lend me some money, _____ .

4. Will you dance with me _____ ?

Where's Your Perfect Nightclub?

Track 45

Each decade in the United States, a different dance craze seems to sweep the nation. In the 90s, swing music saw a resurgence in popularity. As a result, swing dance nightclubs opened up all over the place. People even took swing dance classes so that they could display their new dance skills at the nightclubs on Friday and Saturday nights. Like all fads, swing dancing eventually faded away and was replaced by an interest in salsa dancing, which became very popular in the early 2000s.

Some genres of dance music have had longer staying power than the fads of swing and salsa. Electronic dance music, or EDM, has been very popular with young people since it was first introduced in the 1980s. Nightclubs exist where those who enjoy this kind of music can go to dance the night away to their favorite DJ's music. DJs who started playing music in small EDM nightclubs have gone on to become world famous and sell multi-platinum albums.

As you can see, there are so many kinds of nightclubs in the United States that it would be impossible to discuss all of them. What is central to a nightclub is the music genre and the fans of that genre it decides to cater to. The lighting, the interior design, and the atmosphere it attempts to create all center around the music. If you decide to go to a nightclub in America, think about what kind of music you enjoy. There is sure to be the perfect nightclub for you!

Read the article. Check T for true or F for false.

1. Salsa dancing saw a resurgence in popularity in the 90s in the USA.   T ☐ / F ☐
2. Electronic dance music remains popular, although it started in the 80s.   T ☐ / F ☐
3. Nowadays, DJs don't play music in nightclubs in the USA.   T ☐ / F ☐

Fast Food

Track 46

Fast Food: A Quick History in America

Americans love their fast-food restaurants. Most of the iconic fast-food brands the world has become familiar with originated in the United States. In addition to the traditional "burger and fries" restaurants such as McDonald's, Burger King, and Wendy's, a variety of other American fast-food chains exist. For example, there are Mexican fast-food chains like Taco Bell and Chipotle, popular sandwich restaurants like Subway and Chick-Fil-A, and various fried chicken restaurants like KFC and Popeyes Chicken.

Discuss the following questions.

1. Do you like to eat fast food? If yes, what's your favorite fast-food restaurant?
2. What kinds of fast-food restaurants are there in your country?
3. Is fast food cheaper or more expensive than eating at home in your country?

Fast-food restaurants gained popularity in the 60s and 70s as women gained more independence and went from being stay-at-home moms to professionals in the workplace. Wives and mothers no longer had time to prepare meals for their husbands and children, so grabbing burgers, fries, and soft drinks on the way home from work seemed like the perfect solution to the problem.

In recent decades, as the number of single-parent households has increased, more and more families have had to rely on fast-food restaurants as their main sources of nutrition because of their convenience and affordability. The downside of this, however, is that obesity, diabetes, and heart disease have also increased. These poor health outcomes may also be a function of the current portion sizes, which are much larger than they were in the 70s and 80s.

Conversation ① *Ordering at a Fast-food Restaurant*

A In some fast-food restaurants in America, you can still order from an actual person instead of from an automated touchscreen. You may also ask the worker for substitutions or modifications to your order, but make sure he or she understands what you are asking for, or you might find yourself disappointed when you look at your tray of food. This is a conversation between a woman and a fast-food worker. Listen and practice the conversation with a partner.

Jane is purchasing a meal at a fast-food restaurant.

Clerk Welcome to Burger Brothers! How can I help you?

Jane I'd like a number 3, please.

Clerk So that's one spicy chicken sandwich, a large fries, and a soft drink. What kind of soft drink do you want?

Jane Actually, I'd like to substitute the soft drink with a black coffee. Is that possible?

Clerk Sure. Black coffee. No soft drink. Would you like to supersize your fries?

Jane No, thanks, but I'd like to get my spicy chicken sandwich without tomatoes.

Clerk Spicy chicken sandwich, no tomatoes, large fries, and black coffee. Anything else?

Jane No, I think that's it.

Clerk $5.79, please.

Jane Here's my credit card.

Clerk Here's your receipt. Please wait over there, and your food will arrive shortly.

Jane Thanks.

⊘ **Words to Know** spicy soft drink supersize

B Practice the conversation with a partner. Use the information in the box below.

A ¹ ....

B So that's one ² ...., a large fries, and a soft drink. What kind of soft drink do you want?

A Actually, I'd like to substitute the soft drink with a ³ .... Is that possible?

B Yes, but it will cost you an extra seventy-five cents.

1	2	3
Can I get a number 3, please?	cheeseburger	chocolate milk
Can I have a number 4, please?	chicken nugget set	vanilla milkshake
I'd like a number 6, please.	chicken fajita	hot chocolate

Language Focus

A Fast-food restaurants in the United States want to make the customers happy, so do not hesitate to ask for substitutions or modifications. Here are some expressions you can use in order to ask for substitutions when dining at an American fast-food restaurant.

Making Substitutions
I'd like to **substitute** French fries with potato chips.
Can I **exchange** the soft drink for an orange juice?
Can I have a green salad **instead of** French fries?
May I **replace** the soft drink with a strawberry milkshake?

B Write sentences requesting substitutions for the items.

1. French fries → hash browns

_____

2. soft drink → hot chocolate

_____

3. cheeseburger → veggie burger

_____

4. soft drink → chocolate milkshake

_____

Speak Out | Pair Work

Find a partner. Take turns ordering set meals, but ask your partner for substitutions.

Set Meals
1. Hamburger + French fries + soft drink
2. Cheeseburger + hash browns + chocolate milkshake
3. Chickenburger + potato chips + vanilla milkshake
4. Cheeseburger + side salad + iced coffee
5. Burrito + nachos + soft drink

A *How can I help you?*
B *I'd like a number 1 set meal, but I'd like to replace the French fries with hash browns.*

Conversation ② *At the Drive-thru*

⊚ Track 48

A Cars are a very important aspect of transportation in the United States. Because of this, fast-food restaurants created the drive-thru. At the drive-thru, you can purchase your meal while sitting in your car and ordering through a speaker that sits just outside the driver's side window. You then go to the drive-up window where you can pay and receive your meal. Do fast-food restaurants have drive-thru sections in your country? Listen and practice the conversation with a partner.

Mingyu is buying fast food by using the drive-thru.

Clerk	Welcome to Burger Brothers. How may I help you?
Mingyu	Can I get one number 3, please?
Clerk	One number 3. What kind of soft drink would you like?
Mingyu	Can I substitute the soft drink with a vanilla milkshake?
Clerk	Yes, for an ex… *(unintelligible)*
Mingyu	I'm sorry, but I didn't catch that.
Clerk	You can substitute the soft drink with a milkshake for an extra dollar.
Mingyu	Okay, that's fine.
Clerk	Anything else, sir?
Mingyu	No, that'll do it.
Clerk	Your total comes to seven … *(unintelligible)*
Mingyu	I'm sorry, but I couldn't hear you.
Clerk	$7.89. Please drive around to the next window.

⊘ **Words to Know**   drive-thru   catch   extra   come to

B Practice the conversation with a partner. Use the information in the box below.

A Can I substitute the soft drink with ¹ _____ ?

B Yes, for an ex… *(unintelligible)*

A I'm sorry, but ² _____

B You can substitute the soft drink with ¹ _____ for an extra ³ _____ .

1	2	3
a chocolate milkshake	I didn't catch that.	$1.50
a root beer float	could you say that again?	$2.00
an iced tea	could you repeat that?	fifty cents

Language Focus

A The drive-thru sections of fast-food restaurants are notorious for having poor sound systems. At times, it can be difficult to understand the fast-food worker or vice-versa. Here are some examples of expressions we use to ask for repetition.

Asking for Repetition	
Could you repeat that, please?	Could you say that again, please?
Could you say that one more time, please?	I'm sorry, but I didn't catch that.
I'm sorry, but I missed that.	I'm sorry, but I didn't/couldn't hear you.

B Complete the conversation by using the expressions from the chart. Then, practice it with a partner.

A I'd like a chee… *(unintelligible)*

B _____

A Yes, I said I would like a cheeseburger.

B Anything to … *(unintelligible)*

A _____

B Anything to drink?

A Yes. I'd like a large co… *(unintelligible)*

B _____

A I'd like a large cola, please.

B Okay, so that's one cheeseburger and one large cola. Your total comes to four … *(unintelligible)*

A _____

B That's $4.75.

Speak Out | Pair Work

Find a partner. Then, ask your partner to lend you something from his or her desk. Ask in such a low whisper that he or she cannot understand you. Repeat your request more loudly when your partner uses one of the expressions above. Switch roles and repeat the exercise several times.

A *Can I borrow your eraser?*
B *I'm sorry, but I didn't catch that.*
A *(loud volume) Can I borrow your eraser?*
B *Sure. You can use it.*

Conversation ③ *At the Deli*

🅢Track 49

A In some sandwich shops in the United States, you can build your own sandwiches by choosing the kind of bread you want to use for your sandwich, what kinds of meat and cheese you want on it, and what kinds of vegetables and condiments you would like on it. Listen and practice the conversation with a partner.

Julie is ordering a sandwich at a deli.

Clerk   How can I help you?

Julie   I'd like a turkey sandwich.

Clerk   What kind of bread would you like?

Julie   Wheat.

Clerk   Do you want cheese on that?

Julie   Just a little cheddar.

Clerk   Okay. And what kinds of vegetables would you like?

Julie   I'd like a lot of lettuce, onions, and tomato slices.

Clerk   No problem.

Julie   I'm sorry, but there are too many onions on my sandwich. Can you take a few off?

Clerk   Sure. And which condiments would you like?

Julie   Give me a lot of mustard and mayonnaise.

Clerk   Okay.

Julie   Whoa! I'm sorry, but that's too much mayonnaise. Can you take a little off?

Clerk   No problem. Anything else?

Julie   Just a little salt and pepper.

⊘ **Words to Know**   wheat   cheddar   slices

B Practice the conversation with a partner. Use the information in the box below.

A   What kinds of vegetables would you like?

B   I'd like a lot of olives, onions, and [1] ....

A   No problem.

B   I'm sorry, but there [2] .... on my sandwich. Can you take a [3] .... off?

1	2	3
lettuce	are too many olives	couple
avocado	is too much avocado	little
tomato slices	are too many onions	few

Language Focus

A Here are several expressions that can help you order your sandwich exactly how you want it. Look at the chart.

a lot of (countable/uncountable nouns)	**a little** (uncountable nouns)	**a few** (countable nouns)
I'd like **a lot of** olives.	Just **a little** mayonnaise.	I'd like **a few** pickles.
Give me **a lot of** mustard.	Give me **a little** salt.	Give me **a few** tomato slices.
Can I have **a lot of** lettuce?	Just **a little** avocado.	Just **a few** peppers, please.

too much (uncountable nouns)		**too many** (countable nouns)
That's **too much** salt.		I'm sorry, but there are **too many** onions on it.
That's **too much** mustard.		There are **too many** jalapeno peppers.
I don't want **too much** ketchup on it.		There are **too many** tomato slices.

B Fill in the blanks with the correct expressions from the chart.

1. I'm sorry, but there are _____ olives on my sandwich.

2. Just _____ salt and pepper, please. Not too much.

3. Give me _____ tomato slices. I love them!

4. Whoa! That's _____ mayonnaise. I'd like a little less, please.

5. Can I have _____ more pickles? It's almost perfect.

Speak Out | Pair Work

Find a partner. Take turns ordering a sandwich by using the sandwich items chart below. Use the expressions above to explain to your partner exactly how you want your sandwich.

bread	meat	cheese	vegetable	sauce
white	ham	American	lettuce	mayonnaise
wheat	turkey	mozzarella	tomato slices	mustard
sourdough	bacon	cheddar	olives	chipotle sauce

A *What kind of bread do you want?*
B *I'd like wheat bread, please. With a lot of turkey and a little mozzarella cheese.*
A *How about vegetables? What would you like?*
B *I'd like a little lettuce, a few tomato slices, and lots of olives. I love them!*
A *Do you want any sauce?*
B *Give me lots of mustard but no mayo or ketchup.*

Wrap It Up

Complete the sentences by using the words in the box.

| supersize | spicy | comes to | catch | slices |

1. Would you like to _____ the French fries and soft drink?
2. Your total _____ $12.18, sir.
3. I'm sorry. I didn't _____ that. Could you repeat it?
4. How many tomato _____ would you like on your sandwich?
5. I'd like a lot of chili peppers. I like my sandwiches _____ .

Situation Talk

A **Role-play the following situation with a partner.**

Role **A**

You are a worker at a fast-food restaurant.

1. Ask B how you can help him or her.
2. Ask B if he or she would like to supersize his or her fries.
3. Ask B what kind of soft drink he or she wants.
4. Tell B that it is okay, but he or she must pay one extra dollar.
5. Tell B his or her total is $7.48.
6. Tell B the price again.

Role **B**

You are a customer at a fast-food restaurant.

1. Order a number 2 set meal from B.
2. Tell A that you do not want to supersize your fries.
3. Ask A if you can substitute the soft drink with a milkshake.
4. Tell A that that is fine.
5. Tell A that you didn't catch that.

B **Find a partner. Then, imagine you are a customer at a sandwich shop and your partner is a worker there. Order a sandwich as you like. Take turns.**

Cho's Sandwich Shop

Build Your Own Sandwich!

white   whole wheat   rye

spinach   tomato   lettuce   pickles

cheese   ham   bacon   egg

KETCHUP   MUSTARD   MAYONNAISE

Do You Usually Supersize It?

Track 50

At fast-food restaurant headquarters in the United States, executives are always trying to predict cultural trends. For example, in the 90s, people wanted to feel like they were getting a good deal, so fast-food restaurants introduced the idea of supersizing meals. This included an exorbitant number of fries and an enormous soft drink to go along with a burger or sandwich. The problem with supersizing your meal is that you are also supersizing the calories. At a time when the overall health of the American public was in decline because of an obesity epidemic and an increase in the number of diabetes cases, supersized meals for a few extra cents sounded like a bargain but was actually hurting people.

In the 2000s, people began to understand that consuming too much sugar, fat, and carbohydrates was not good for them, so fast-food restaurants started offering healthier options on their menus like salads and low-calorie wraps. Around this time, the dollar menu also became a thing. You could choose regularly sized individual items such as a simple hamburger, a small French fries, and a regular-sized soda. Additional items like chicken wraps and chili became available at some fast-food restaurants, so now eating at a fast-food restaurant did not have to be as unhealthy as it had been before because there were healthier options available.

We have to remember that fast-food restaurants exist to earn money. They are not necessarily interested in the long-term health outcomes of their customers. We have to protect ourselves by insisting they give us options that are less harmful to our health in order to continue having us as customers at their fast-food restaurants.

Read the article. Answer these questions.

1. Why did fast-food restaurants begin offering customers the option to supersize their meals in the 90s?
2. What was the problem with supersizing meals at fast-food restaurants?
3. When did fast-food restaurants start offering healthier options on their menus?

Holidays in America

Track 51

The Holiday Season

The holiday season begins on Thanksgiving in the United States. Thanksgiving is always celebrated on the fourth Thursday in November, so the date changes slightly from year to year. The holiday season lasts for approximately a month and ends on the 1st of January, which is New Year's Day. Traditionally, Thanksgiving was a harvest festival in which people gave thanks for the summer's bountiful crops.

In modern times, it is a time for families to get together and to give thanks for the positive things happening in their lives. Most families cook a turkey on Thanksgiving, and it is accompanied by other side dishes such as mashed potatoes, stuffing, cranberry sauce, and pumpkin pie. The Friday after Thanksgiving is nicknamed Black Friday as many people begin Christmas shopping on this day.

Discuss the following questions.

1. Do you celebrate Christmas and Thanksgiving in your country?
2. What is the most important holiday in your country? Why?
3. Do you celebrate a day of independence in your country? If so, which country did yours gain independence from?

Christmas occurs on the 25th of December. Traditionally, it was a Christian religious holiday celebrating the birth of Jesus Christ, but many non-religious Americans also celebrate the holiday by enjoying a meal together with their family members. One of the most popular aspects of Christmas is exchanging gifts with friends and family members. This is the reason why so many shoppers rush to shopping malls and supermarkets on Black Friday. They want to find the best bargains.

Conversation ① *Thanksgiving Dinner*

A A popular Thanksgiving tradition in America is to go around the table in a circle as each person says what he or she is thankful for. This is an example of a husband and wife saying what they are thankful for. Listen and practice the conversation with a partner.

Garret's family is having Thanksgiving dinner.

Garret Attention, everyone! It's time to raise our glasses and say what we're thankful for this year.

Ashley Why don't you go first?

Garret Okay. I want to start by saying I'm thankful for my wonderful wife, Ashley, and our two boys, Jack and Zach. I'm also thankful for my two wonderful parents. I love you, Mom and Dad. Finally, I'm thankful for this delicious meal that we are about to enjoy together. Ashley, the turkey looks absolutely amazing.

Ashley Thank you, honey. I followed your mother's recipe.

Garret Thanks, too, Mom! Now, it's your turn, Ashley.

Ashley I'm so thankful for my loving husband, Garret, our beautiful children, and my delightful in-laws. But I'm also really thankful for the Luis Vuitton purse Garret bought me for Christmas.

Garret What? That was supposed to be a surprise. I was going to give you that purse on Christmas.

Ashley I found it in the back of the closet while I was cleaning yesterday. I love it!

Garret Well, at least I'm good at choosing gifts.

Ashley You're just terrible at hiding them.

⊘ **Words to Know**   thankful   delightful   in-laws   surprise

B Practice the conversation with a partner. Use the information in the box below.

A It's time to raise our glasses and say what we're ¹ _____ this year.

B Why don't you go first?

A I want to say that I'm thankful for ² _____ . How about you?

B I'm grateful for ³ _____ .

1	2	3
grateful for	my good health	my terrific wife
appreciative of	my amazing husband	my loving parents
thankful for	my new job	this wonderful meal

Language Focus

A English speakers often put positive adjectives before nouns when they want to stress the quality or importance of the noun. Look at the chart.

Adjectives		Nouns	
amazing	brilliant	family	friends
excellent	good	parents	grandparents
great	loving	husband/wife	children/child/son/daughter
magnificent	wonderful	health/job/career/education	
I'm thankful for my wonderful family and friends. I'm appreciative of my good health this year.		I'm very grateful for my loving children.	

B Look at the pictures. Then, write sentences of gratitude by using the adjectives and nouns from the chart. Answers may vary.

1.

I'm thankful for my
wonderful parents.

2.

3.

4.

5.

6.

Speak Out | Class Activity

Ask three classmates what they are thankful for this year. Then, write their answers in the blanks.

Student 1 I'm thankful for _____.

Student 2 I'm grateful for _____.

Student 3 I'm appreciative of _____.

A *What are you appreciative of this year?*
B *I'm appreciative of my amazing boyfriend.*

Conversation ② *Opening Presents on Christmas Morning*

Track 53

A It is common for American families to spend the entire day together on Christmas. In the morning, they often get together to open presents from under the Christmas tree. This is a conversation between a husband and wife opening each other's Christmas presents. Listen and practice the conversation with a partner.

Kristen and Caleb are opening each other's Christmas presents.

Caleb What is it?

Kristen You have to open it to find out.

Caleb It feels heavy, but the box isn't very big.

Kristen Open it!

Caleb It's smaller than a book, but it's bigger than a phone.

Kristen Just open it already!

Caleb Okay, I will. Oh, my gosh! It's a Bluetooth gaming controller! Thank you. I love it.

Kristen You're welcome. I know your old controller is worn out.

Caleb Open my present now.

Kristen It's not very heavy, but the box is kind of large. Is it a sweater?

Caleb Just open it.

Kristen It's another box.

Caleb Open the second box.

Kristen It's a smaller box?

Caleb Open that one.

Kristen Oh, my goodness! It's a diamond ring. It's so pretty!

✅ Words to Know   controller   worn out   diamond

B Practice the conversation with a partner. Use the information in the box below.

A Open my present.

B It's ¹ _____ than a book, but it's ² _____ than a ³ _____ .

A Just open it already!

B Okay, I will. Oh, my gosh! It's a ⁴ _____ ! Thank you. I love it.

1	2	3	4
bigger	smaller	laptop	tablet
smaller	larger	ring	smartwatch
heavier	lighter	bowling ball	Bluetooth speaker

Language Focus

A Let's learn about comparative adjectives. Look at the chart.

Comparative Adjectives	
small → small**er than**	big → big**ger than**
short → short**er than**	long → long**er than**
heavy → heav**ier than**	light → light**er than**
thin → thin**ner than**	thick → thick**er than**
expensive → **more** expensive **than**	cheap → cheap**er than**

B Use the words below to write sentences which describe some unnamed objects.

1. big/coin – small/book *It's bigger than a coin but smaller than a book.*

2. short/umbrella – long/boot

3. heavy/watch – light/phone

4. thin/dictionary – thick/newspaper

5. expensive/smartwatch – cheap / diamond necklace

Speak Out | Pair Work

Find a partner. Then, make sentences about one of the items by using comparatives. Let your partner guess which item you are referring to.

A *It's smaller than a book, but it's bigger than air pods.*
B *Is it a smartphone?*

Conversation ③ *The 4th of July*

Track 54

A The 4th of July is a day commemorating the ratification of the Declaration of Independence on July 4, 1776, and a day of remembrance for those who fought for American independence from the English during the American Revolution. The day is often celebrated by getting together with family and friends, barbecuing, and watching fireworks displays. Listen and practice the conversation with a partner.

Randall and Stephanie are talking about their plans for the 4th of July.

Randall Are you going to go to the city's fireworks display on the 4th of July?

Stephanie I'm not sure.

Randall Why not? The city always puts on an amazing show.

Stephanie I know. We might be going to my uncle's house on the 4th. He lives on a lake and has a boat.

Randall That sounds like fun.

Stephanie We're going to go waterskiing during the day, and then at night, we're going to have a barbecue. After that, he's going to set off some fireworks that he bought.

Randall Whoa. I hope he's careful.

Stephanie He's pretty careful about who he lets near the fireworks. It won't be as exciting as the city's fireworks display, but at least I'll have a front-row seat.

Randall I can't argue with your logic. Well, have fun.

Stephanie Thanks. You, too.

✓ **Words to Know**   fireworks   set off   argue   logic

B Practice the conversation with a partner. Use the information in the box below.

A What are you going to do on the 4th of July?

B I'm going to my ¹ _____ house. We're going to go ² _____ during the day, and at night, he's going to set off some fireworks that he bought. How about you?

A My family is going to have a picnic at the park. The food won't be as ³ _____ as last year's because my aunt is sick and can't come. The fireworks will be great though.

1	2	3
grandfather's	swimming	delicious
friend's	fishing	amazing
cousin's	tubing	enjoyable

Language Focus

A Native English speakers will sometimes use this construction to compare two things: **not as (adjective) as ~**. Look at the chart.

not as (adjective) as
Our boat **isn't as fast as** their boat. = Their boat **is faster than** ours.
My uncle's fireworks **aren't as exciting as** the city's fireworks display. = The city's fireworks display **is more exciting than** my uncle's.
Our barbecue party **won't be as extravagant as** the Miller family's barbecue. = The Miller family's barbecue **will be more extravagant than** ours.
The beer at my cousin's party **won't be as expensive as** the beer at my grandfather's party. = The beer at my grandfather's party **will be more expensive than** the beer at my cousin's.

B Make each pair of sentences have the same meaning.

1. Watching movies is more exciting than reading books.

= Reading books _____ watching movies.

2. The food at our neighbor's house party will be fancier than the food at our house party.

= The food at our house party _____ the food at our neighbor's.

3. The water in our swimming pool is warmer than the water in the lake.

= _____

4. The capital's fireworks display will be more extravagant than the fireworks display in our city.

= _____

Speak Out | Pair Work

Share your opinions about the activities in the chart with a partner by using the grammar from above.

A	B
swimming in the pool	swimming in the lake
waterskiing	tubing / banana boating
amusement park	zoo
picnic	barbecue
playing soccer	playing basketball

Swimming in the pool won't be as interesting as swimming in the lake.

Wrap It Up

Vocabulary Check
Match the words with their correct definitions.

1. in-laws •
2. surprise •
3. worn out •
4. fireworks •
5. argue •

• ⓐ so old or damaged that it cannot be used anymore

• ⓑ to disagree with what somebody says

• ⓒ the parents of your husband or wife

• ⓓ something unexpected; a shock

• ⓔ a device which contains gunpowder and other chemicals which results in a beautiful light display

Situation Talk

A **Role-play the following situation with a partner.**

You are having Thanksgiving dinner at a friend's house.

1. Thank B for inviting you to Thanksgiving dinner. Compliment B on the turkey.
2. Tell B that you would like more turkey.
3. Say what you are thankful for this year and thank your friend B.

Your friend is having Thanksgiving dinner at your house.

1. Tell A that he or she is welcome. Ask A if he or she wants any more turkey.
2. Get everyone's attention. Tell everyone that you would like them to say what they are thankful for this year. Ask A to go first.
3. Say thank you. Say what you are thankful for.

B **Find a partner. Then, answer the questions with true information about your partner's and your items. After that, write comparative sentences by using the "not as (adjective) as" construction.**

You	Questions	Your Partner
	How old is your bag?	
	How heavy is your bag?	
	How expensive is your computer?	
	How new is your cell phone?	
	How colorful is your shirt?	

My bag isn't as old as my partner's bag. / My partner's bag isn't as old as my bag.

Some Smaller Holidays

Track 55

Christmas, Thanksgiving, and New Year's Day are the three biggest holidays in the United States and make up the holiday season. However, there are a few other holidays outside of the holiday season we can discuss. The most historically important holiday for Americans is the 4th of July. On this day, Americans do not go to work because it is a national holiday. Americans like to grill hamburgers, bratwurst, and hot dogs on this day. In the evening, when the sun goes down, cities put on fireworks displays that represent the battles which took place during the Revolutionary War.

There is another popular holiday which is not considered a national holiday because people go to work on this day if it falls on a weekday. This holiday is called Halloween, and it takes place on October 31. Its name means All Hallowed Eve or the Evening Before All Saints Day (November 1). Halloween used to be a children's holiday. On this day, children dressed up in costumes and went trick-or-treating, which involved going door to door in their neighborhoods and asking for candy.

These days, children continue to enjoy trick-or-treating, but adults, especially college-age adults, also commonly enjoy the holiday by having Halloween parties. Guests at the parties dress up in costumes and celebrate the evening together by drinking alcoholic beverages. Although most children outgrow trick-or-treating by age 11 or 12, attending a college Halloween party is not considered immature, so do not feel embarrassed to don a costume and to attend one. Besides, you would not want to be the only person there without a costume!

Read the article. Check T for true or F for false.
1. The three most popular holidays in the USA are Thanksgiving, Christmas, and Halloween. T ☐ / F ☐
2. Halloween takes place the day before All Saints Day. T ☐ / F ☐
3. These days, adults enjoy Halloween as much as children do. T ☐ / F ☐

Cooking for Fun

American Home Cooking

Track 56

In the 1950s and 1960s, it was common for American women to stay at home and to prepare meals for their husbands and children. In the past four to five decades, however, the convenience of precooked, microwavable meals and fast food has reduced the need for family members to prepare home-cooked meals from scratch.

Although cooking out of necessity has declined, a number of Americans now choose to cook just for the enjoyment of it. This is partly the result of the popularity of cooking shows. Celebrity chefs like Gordon Ramsay, Jamie Oliver, and Rachael Ray have inspired fans to take out their pots and pans and to attempt to follow recipes to completion in their own kitchens.

Another interesting fact about cooking in the USA is that there is not one cuisine that can be considered uniquely American. The United States is a melting pot of many different cultures, nationalities, and ethnicities. In fact, most families in the United States identify more strongly with their descendants' cuisines than they do with their descendants' languages or cultural practices. It is particularly common to see Americans cook foods related to their ancestral homelands on holidays.

Discuss the following questions.

1. Do you enjoy cooking meals at home?

2. What kinds of dishes can you cook? What is your specialty?

3. Who usually does the cooking in your home?

Conversation ❶ *Cooking Pasta Together*

🎧 Track 57

A These days, men in the USA are expected to do their fair share of the household chores. Because of this cultural change, it is not uncommon to find men in the kitchen preparing home-cooked meals. Sometimes couples cook together just for the fun of it. This is a conversation between a couple cooking together. Listen and practice the conversation with a partner.

Philip and Dawn are preparing a pasta dinner at home.

Philip   So, what should I do first?

Dawn   Chop up these tomatoes, onions, peppers, and garlic.

Philip   Got it.

Dawn   I'll boil the water and cook the pasta.

Philip   Don't we need a can of tomato paste?

Dawn   Yes, there's one in the cupboard. Can you grab it?

Philip   Is it in here?

Dawn   No, the cupboard next to that one.

Philip   Here it is.

(sounds of chopping and boiling water)

Philip   I'm done chopping up these vegetables. What should I do next?

Dawn   Put some oil in a saucepan and fry them over the stove. Next, add some tomato paste, sugar, salt, and pepper. Finally, stir the sauce slowly until it starts to bubble.

Philip   I can handle that.

Dawn   When the noodles are ready, we'll be able to enjoy some homemade spaghetti!

Philip   Great!

⊘ Words to Know   cupboard   grab   saucepan   handle

B   Practice the conversation with a partner. Use the information in the box below.

A   I'm done chopping up these ¹ _____ . What should I do next?

B   Put some oil in a saucepan and fry them over the stove. Next, add some ² _____ . Finally, stir the ³ _____ slowly until it starts to bubble.

A   I can handle that.

1	2	3
potatoes and onions	water and curry powder	curry
carrots and onions	chicken broth	soup
carrots and potatoes	beef and a little beef broth	stew

Language Focus

A When following a recipe in English, you must be familiar with some common verbs related to cooking methods. Look at the chart.

Cooking Instructions

| add | pour | stir | chop up | boil | fry |

B Look at the pictures and write the correct words.

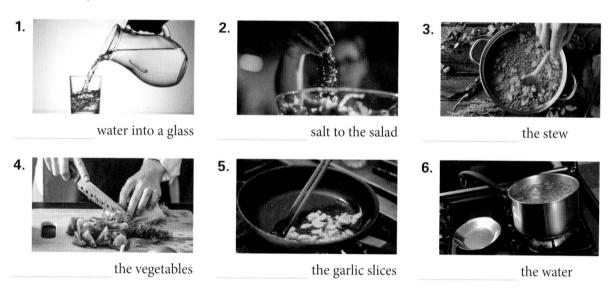

1. _____ water into a glass

2. _____ salt to the salad

3. _____ the stew

4. _____ the vegetables

5. _____ the garlic slices

6. _____ the water

Speak Out | Pair Work

Find a partner. Then, create a recipe for a dish with your partner. When you are finished, share your recipe with the class.

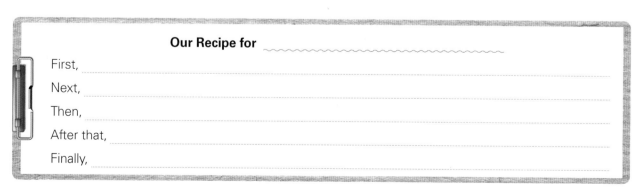

Our Recipe for _____

First, _____

Next, _____

Then, _____

After that, _____

Finally, _____

Here is our recipe for two-egg instant noodles. First, pour water into a pot. Next, boil the water. Then, add the packet of flavoring to the water. After that, add two eggs to the soup. Finally, add the noodles to the soup and stir them.

Conversation ② *Baking Chocolate Chip Cookies*

A As much as some Americans enjoy cooking, many also enjoy baking. Almost all American kitchens have ovens, so baking is a popular hobby for a lot of people. This is a conversation between a couple baking cookies together. Listen and practice the conversation with a partner.

Myrna and George are baking chocolate chip cookies at home.

Myrna What do we need to do first, George?

George It says here that we need to preheat the oven to 350 degrees Fahrenheit.

Myrna Done. What's next?

George Mix three cups of flour, one teaspoon of baking soda, and one teaspoon of salt in a bowl and set the bowl aside.

Myrna Okay… all done. What should I do now?

George Add a cup of sugar, two teaspoons of vanilla, and a cup of butter into the other bowl. Then, crack two eggs into the bowl and beat them until all of the contents in the bowl are fluffy.

Myrna Is this fluffy enough?

George Yes, that's perfect. Now, pour the contents of the first bowl into the second bowl and mix everything together.

Myrna It's really sticky. My arm's getting tired.

George Here, I'll help you. Okay, that's good.

Myrna Anything else?

George Yeah. I want you to dump that whole bag of chocolate chips into the bowl and mix it all together.

⊘ **Words to Know**   preheat   flour   crack   beat   fluffy

---

B Practice the conversation with a partner. Use the information in the box below.

A What do we need to do first?

B It says here that we need to preheat the oven to ¹ _____ degrees Fahrenheit.

A ² _____ . What's next?

B Mix ³ _____ , baking soda, and salt in a bowl and set the bowl aside.

1	2	3
450	I did it	whole wheat flour
375	Finished	gluten-free flour
425	Done	cornmeal

Language Focus

A Understanding measurements in a recipe which is written in English can be very difficult if you do not know the conversions. Below is a chart of the most common measurements used in recipes in America and conversions to the metric system, which is the most common system used worldwide.

Measurements and Conversions						
Volume		Weight		Temperature		Easy Conversions
USA	Metric	USA	Metric	Fahrenheit	Celsius	3 tsp = 1 tbsp
1 teaspoon	5 milliliters	1/2 ounce	15 grams	250	120	8 tbsp = 1/2 cup
1 tablespoon	15 milliliters	1 ounce	30 grams	350	180	12 tbsp = 3/4 cup
1/2 cup	125 milliliters	1 pound	450 grams	400	200	16 tbsp = 1 cup
1 cup	250 milliliters	2 1/4 pounds	1 kilogram	450	230	16 ounces = 1 pound

B Complete the sentences with the correct measurements.

1. **A** The recipe calls for three cups of flour. How many milliliters is that?

   B It's _____ milliliters of flour.

2. **A** We need to preheat the oven to 400 degrees Fahrenheit.

   B Okay. That means _____ degrees Celsius.

3. **A** If we are going to make a large batch of dough, we need to buy at least ten pounds of flour.

   B How much is that in kilograms?

   A Let me see. That would be _____ kilograms.

4. **A** I need to add one cup of sugar, but I can't find the measuring cup. Can I use a measuring spoon instead?

   B Sure. Just add _____ tablespoons.

Speak Out | Pair Work

Find a partner. Then, imagine you are baking together, but you do not know the American measurement system. Ask your partner to make conversions for the measurements.

INGREDIENTS				
2 cups cornmeal	3 ounces sugar	3 tsp salt	2 tbsp butter	4 1/2 pounds flour
milliliters?	grams?	tablespoons?	milliliters?	kilograms?

A *I need two cups of cornmeal. How many milliliters is that?*
B *It's 500 milliliters.*

Conversation ③ *Asking for a Recipe*

🔊 Track 59

A **While living in the United States, you might decide to invite friends over to your home for a meal. You might also find yourself in need of a good recipe. Do not forget to ask your guests about any possible food allergies or sensitivities that they might have. This is a conversation in which one friend asks another for a good recipe. Listen and practice the conversation with a partner.**

Justine is asking her friend Erin if she has a recipe she can use for a dinner party.

Justine Hey, Erin. I'm having some friends over for dinner on Friday. Would you like to come?

Erin I'd love to.

Justine I have a problem though.

Erin What's that?

Justine I need a good recipe for a main dish, but it has to be gluten-free.

Erin I've got a great recipe for lasagna.

Justine Really? Is it gluten-free?

Erin No, but you could substitute gluten-free lasagna noodles for regular ones.

Justine Okay, so I need gluten-free lasagna noodles. What other ingredients do I need?

Erin In addition to the noodles, you'll need some marinara sauce, minced beef, ricotta and mozzarella cheese, spinach, onions, garlic, and basil. It's that simple.

Justine Oh, it sounds wonderful. Do you think you could email me the recipe?

Erin Absolutely. I'll send it to you as soon as we're done talking.

✅ **Words to Know** gluten-free ingredients minced

B **Practice the conversation with a partner. Use the information in the box below.**

A I need a good recipe for a ¹ _____ , but it has to be gluten-free.

B I've got a great recipe for ² _____ . I can email it to you.

A Really? Is it gluten-free?

B No, but you could substitute gluten-free ³ _____ .

1	2	3
dessert	tiramisu	flour for regular flour
starter	canapés	bread for regular bread
main dish	pasta	noodles for regular noodles

Language Focus

A Look at some of the most common food allergies in the chart.

Most Common Food Allergies

eggs   gluten   milk   peanuts   shellfish   tree nuts

B Fill in the blanks with the correct food allergies from the chart.

1. A I'm going to make some clam chowder. Would you like some?

  B I can't eat clams. I have a _____ allergy.

2. A Would you like an omelet?

  B No, thanks. I'm allergic to _____.

3. A I'm making you a peanut butter and jam sandwich for lunch.

  B Could I have a ham sandwich instead? I'm allergic to _____.

4. A Let's get some vanilla milkshakes.

  B No, thanks. I can't drink _____. I have an allergy.

5. A I'm baking some almond cookies. Would you like to help?

  B I would love to, but I can't be around any _____. I'm allergic to them.

Speak Out | Class Activity

Have your teacher conduct a classroom survey about the food allergies in the chart. Raise your hand if you have the food allergy. Then, find a partner and discuss the results by sharing your answers to the questions below.

	eggs	gluten	milk	peanuts	shellfish	tree nuts
Number of students with a food allergy to …						

1. What was the most common food allergy in the class? Were you surprised by this result?
2. What was the least common food allergy in the class? Were you surprised by this result?
3. Do you have any food allergies? If so, which ones, and are they in the chart?

Wrap It Up

Fill in the blanks with the correct answers.

1. Can you grab the pot from the _____?   ⓐ saucepan   ⓑ cupboard

2. You have to _____ the eggs until they are fluffy.   ⓐ beat   ⓑ preheat

3. Is this pasta _____? I have an allergy.   ⓐ minced   ⓑ gluten-free

4. First, we need to pour some _____ in a bowl.   ⓐ crack   ⓑ flour

5. We should add the _____ pork to the sauce.   ⓐ minced   ⓑ ingredients

Situation Talk

A   **Role-play the following situation with a partner.**

Role **A**	Role **B**
You are helping your husband or wife cook a meal.	*Your husband or wife is helping you cook a meal.*
1. Ask B how you can help him or her.	1. Tell A that you would like him or her to chop up some carrots, potatoes, and onions.
2. Tell B that you have finished chopping up the carrots, potatoes, and onions. Ask B what you should do next.	2. Say "Thank you." to A. Tell A to pour some water into a pot and boil it.
3. Tell B that the water is boiling.	3. Tell A to put the carrots, potatoes, and onions into the boiling water.

B   **Use the Internet to search for a cookie recipe that looks delicious to you. Write the ingredients you need to make the cookies in the left-hand column and the baking instructions in the right-hand column. Then, find a partner and share your recipe with him or her.**

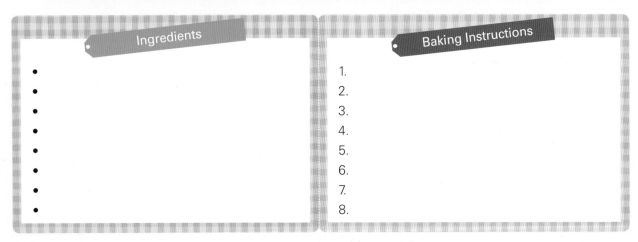

Ingredients

-
-
-
-
-
-
-

Baking Instructions

1.
2.
3.
4.
5.
6.
7.
8.

Eating at Home in America

Track 60

In many countries, it is cheaper to eat out than it is to buy groceries and to cook a meal at home. Unfortunately, the United States is not one of these countries. If you want to eat a nice meal for a reasonable price, you should go to the supermarket, purchase some fruit, vegetables, and meat, and prepare your own meal at home. Since buying groceries is cheaper, those living in the United States need to learn how to make some home-cooked meals.

To do this, there are some essential kitchen items that you should become familiar with. These include an oven, a stove, a microwave, and a crockpot. A crockpot is an electronic device, also known as a slow cooker, which cooks ingredients at a low temperature over a long period of time. For example, an inexpensive piece of meat from the supermarket might be tough and hard to eat when grilled, but when put in a crockpot and left to simmer at a low temperature for several hours, it becomes soft and tender. Americans also rely on a different set of utensils than those visiting the country might be used to. Americans tend to use a fork and knife to cut and eat meat. They use a spoon in order to scoop soup, stew, and other soft foods. Chopsticks are not always available in American homes.

A big difference you might notice about eating a home-cooked meal at a typical American person's house is that each person at the table gets his or her own plate of food. The average family in the United

States might find it unusual to share from multiple plates and pots. Because the USA is such a melting pot of ethnicities, American families with backgrounds from countries in Asia, South America, and the Middle East may have certain cooking devices, utensils, and methods of eating that are different than those of the average American. But that is what makes America an interesting and diverse country.

Read the article. Answer these questions.
1. What should you do if you want to eat a nice meal for a reasonable price in America?
2. What are some essential kitchen items needed for cooking in America?
3. How would a typical American family feel about sharing multiple plates and pots of food?

Answer Key

Unit 01 Greetings from America

Conversation ❶ Language Focus B   p.13

1. Good morning, good afternoon
2. Hello, How are you doing
3. Hey there, How's it going

Conversation ❷ Language Focus B   p.15

1. Ms. / Mrs.	2. Ms.
3. Ms. / Mrs.	4. Mr.
5. Ms. / Miss	

Conversation ❸ Language Focus B   p.17

1. Dr.	2. Dr.
3. Professor	4. Dr.

Wrap It Up Vocabulary Check   p.18

1. starving	2. conduct
3. assignment	4. eager
5. due	

Just So You Know   p.19

1. F	2. T	3. F

Unit 02 Making Small Talk

Conversation ❶ Language Focus B   p.23

1. The weather is nice, isn't it?
2. This is a fun party, isn't it?
3. The traffic was bad this morning, wasn't it?
4. The Toronto Raptors are great this year, aren't they?
5. People love BTS, don't they?

Conversation ❷ Language Focus B   p.25

1. Wasn't the concert loud?
2. Isn't this wedding fun?
3. Didn't the Lakers play well?
4. Isn't it cold?
5. Didn't you love the movie?

Conversation ❸ Language Focus B   p.27

(Answers may vary.)
1. Could you tell me when the game starts?
2. Do you know where I can find cheap apples?
3. May I ask how long you have lived here?

4. Could you tell me what kind of food you like?
5. Do you mind telling me why you are studying English?
6. Could you tell me what the problem is?

Speak Out

(Answers may vary.)
1. Could you tell me where the back of the checkout line is?
2. May I ask where you're from?
3. Do you know what time it is?

Wrap It Up Vocabulary Check   p.28

1. ⓒ	2. ⓔ	3. ⓐ
4. ⓑ	5. ⓓ	

Situation Talk A

1. It is cold, isn't it?
2. May I ask where you're from?
3. Don't you miss it?
4. Living in London is fun, isn't it?
5. Isn't driving everywhere annoying?

Just So You Know   p.29

1. a marital problem, personal finances, politics, and religion
2. a marital problem or personal finances
3. Because the U.S. is a country with deep political divides and has people with strong religious views.

Unit 03 Sit-down Restaurants

Conversation ❶ Language Focus B   p.33

(Answers may vary.)
1. I'll have
2. Are you ready to order
3. I want
4. May I take your order, I'd like

Conversation ❷ Language Focus B   p.35

1. ⓒ	2. ⓓ	3. ⓔ
4. ⓐ	5. ⓑ	

Conversation ❸ Language Focus B   p.37

1. vegan	2. pescatarian
3. ketogenic	4. vegetarian

Wrap It Up Vocabulary Check p.38

1. ⓑ **2.** ⓑ **3.** ⓐ
4. ⓑ **5.** ⓐ

Just So You Know p.39

1. F **2.** F **3.** T

Unit 04 **A Shopper's Paradise**

Conversation ❶ Language Focus B p.43

1. long **2.** short
3. snug / tight **4.** loose / baggy
5. sloppy

Conversation ❷ Language Focus B p.45

(Answers may vary.)
1. I'm sorry, but $35 is too low.
2. Would you consider taking $70 for it?
3. $10? No, that's too low.
4. Would you be willing to sell it for $100?
5. No, that's ridiculous.

Conversation ❸ Language Focus B p.47

1. between **2.** next to
3. behind **4.** across from

Wrap It Up Vocabulary Check p.48

1. snug **2.** deal
3. halfway **4.** condiments
5. aisle

Just So You Know p.49

1. You need the receipt.
2. You should inform the representative which option you prefer.
3. Corporations must raise prices to offset their losses.

Unit 05 **Let's Party!**

Conversation ❶ Language Focus B p.53

(Answers may vary.)
1. Could you pass me the chicken?
2. Do you mind baking some muffins for me?
3. Can you give me a fork?
4. Would you mind showing us how to do it?
5. Could you tell me your name?
6. Can you send me the report via email?

Speak Out

(Answers may vary.)
1. Can you pass me the potatoes?
2. Would you mind giving me a spoon, too?
3. Could you pass me the meatballs?
4. Do you mind giving me some ketchup?

Conversation ❷ Language Focus B p.55

(Answers may vary.)
1. You have to taste this soup!
2. He must try the pasta!
3. They've got to see the parade!
4. You must try this recipe!
5. Kelly has to come to the Christmas party!
6. Minho has got to go to Disneyland when he visits Orlando!

Conversation ❸ Language Focus B p.57

1. Minseong and Jiwoo have studied English together since 2017.
2. Holly and Emily used to be roommates in college.
3. We've known each other since elementary school.
4. I used to work at ABC Company.

Wrap It Up Vocabulary Check p.58

1. ⓒ **2.** ⓓ **3.** ⓑ
4. ⓔ **5.** ⓐ

Just So You Know p.59

1. F **2.** T **3.** F

Unit 06 **Getting Around Town**

Conversation ❶ Language Focus B p.63

1. We go to church once a week.
2. My father washes his car twice a month.
3. Bus number 39 comes every 10 minutes.
4. My parents have a wedding anniversary party every year.

Conversation ❷ Language Focus B p.65

1. Will this bus take me to
2. Does this bus go to
3. can I get to, on this bus

Conversation ❸ Language Focus B p.67

(Answers may vary.)
A. I am going to take the second left. Then, I will go around the block, take a right at Sushi Heaven, and go straight to the Best Hotel.
B. I will take the third left. Then, I will go around the block, turn right at Lobster Palace, and go straight until I am in front of Lobster Palace.

C. I will take a left. Then, I will go straight. I will go past Shoes 4 U. Bob's Bar and Grill will be on my right.

Wrap It Up Vocabulary Check   p.68
1. ⓐ   **2.** ⓑ   **3.** ⓐ
4. ⓑ   **5.** ⓐ

Just So You Know   p.69
1. It remains insufficient for the amount of traffic it carries.
2. There was a public transportation system consisting of streetcars and buses.
3. They have built light rail systems which allow people to drive from their homes to large parking lots located just outside the city.

Unit 07 Entertainment

Conversation ❶ Language Focus B   p.73
driver's license
passport
green card

Conversation ❷ Language Focus B   p.75
1. a quarter to seven
2. half past two
3. twenty to twelve
4. ten past ten

Wrap It Up Vocabulary Check   p.78
1. entire   **2.** convinced
3. sunset   **4.** on the nose
5. sold out

Just So You Know   p.79
1. F   **2.** T   **3.** T

Unit 08 More Than Just Great Coffee

Conversation ❶ Language Focus B   p.83
1. a pinch of salt
2. a dash of chili powder
3. a splash of milk
4. a sprinkle of powdered sugar
5. a drop of honey
6. a packet of brown sugar

Conversation ❷ Language Focus B   p.85
(Answers may vary.)
1. I'm sorry

2. I'm really sorry
3. I apologize for
4. I'm very sorry
5. I'm truly sorry
6. I apologize for

Conversation ❸ Language Focus B   p.87
1. a bottle of wine
2. a pot of water
3. a carton of eggs
4. a can of beer
5. a crate of apples
6. a box of cookies
7. a glass of juice
8. a bag of rice

Wrap It Up Vocabulary Check   p.88
1. ⓒ   **2.** ⓑ   **3.** ⓐ
4. ⓒ   **5.** ⓓ

Just So You Know   p.89
1. You can have as many refills of coffee as you want for the price of one cup.
2. Starbucks
3. Premium coffee chains want their customers to feel sophisticated and proud that they are drinking good coffee.

Unit 09 Bars and Nightclubs

Conversation ❶ Language Focus B   p.93
1. January twenty-fifth, nineteen seventy-seven
2. September fourth, two thousand eight
3. November eleventh, nineteen ninety-nine
4. May fifteenth, two thousand two
5. August thirtieth, two thousand four

Conversation ❷ Language Focus B   p.95
(Answers may vary.)
1. Can I open a tab?
     I'd like to close the tab.
2. I'd like to keep the tab open.
     You can put it on my tab.

Conversation ❸ Language Focus B   p.97
1. I'll pay for the movie if you pay for dinner. /
     If you pay for dinner, I'll pay for the movie.
2. I'll go jogging with you if you wake up early in the morning. / If you wake up early in the morning, I'll go jogging with you.
3. I won't be angry if you tell the truth. /
     If you tell the truth, I won't be angry.

4. I'll buy you a drink next weekend if you lend me your car this weekend. / If you lend me your car this weekend, I'll buy you a drink next weekend.

Wrap It Up Vocabulary Check   p.98

1. ⓑ   **2.** ⓐ   **3.** ⓑ
4. ⓐ   **5.** ⓐ

Just So You Know   p.99

1. F   **2.** T   **3.** F

Unit 10 Fast Food

Conversation ❶ Language Focus B   p.103

(Answers may vary.)
1. I'd like to substitute French fries with hash browns.
2. Can I exchange the soft drink for a hot chocolate?
3. Can I have a veggie burger instead of a cheeseburger?
4. May I replace the soft drink with a chocolate milkshake?

Conversation ❷ Language Focus B   p.105

(Answers may vary.)
Could you repeat that, please?
I'm sorry, but I didn't catch that.
I'm sorry, but could you say that one more time, please?
Could you say that again, please?

Conversation ❸ Language Focus B   p.107

1. too many   **2.** a little
3. a lot of   **4.** too much
5. a few

Wrap It Up Vocabulary Check   p.108

1. supersize   **2.** comes to
3. catch   **4.** slices
5. spicy

Just So You Know   p.109

1. People wanted to feel like they were getting a good deal.
2. poor health outcomes
3. in the 2000s

Unit 11 Holidays in America

Conversation ❶ Language Focus B   p.113

(Answers may vary.)
1. I'm thankful for my wonderful parents.
2. I'm grateful for my amazing job.
3. I'm appreciative of my good health.

4. I'm very grateful for my loving grandparents.
5. I'm thankful for my great friends.
6. I'm appreciative of my excellent education.

Conversation ❷ Language Focus B   p.115

1. It's bigger than a coin but smaller than a book.
2. It's shorter than an umbrella but longer than a boot.
3. It's heavier than a watch but lighter than a phone.
4. It's thinner than a dictionary but thicker than a newspaper.
5. It's more expensive than a smartwatch but cheaper than a diamond necklace.

Conversation ❸ Language Focus B   p.117

1. isn't as exciting as
2. won't be as fancy as
3. The water in the lake isn't as warm as the water in our swimming pool.
4. The fireworks display in our city won't be as extravagant as the capital's fireworks display.

Wrap It Up Vocabulary Check   p.118

1. ⓒ   **2.** ⓓ   **3.** ⓐ
4. ⓔ   **5.** ⓑ

Just So You Know   p.119

1. F   **2.** T   **3.** T

Unit 12 Cooking for Fun

Conversation ❶ Language Focus B   p.123

1. pour   **2.** add
3. stir   **4.** chop up
5. fry   **6.** boil

Conversation ❷ Language Focus B   p.125

1. 750   **2.** 200
3. 4.5   **4.** 16

Speak Out

A I need three ounces of sugar. How many grams is that?
B It's 90 grams.

A I need three teaspoons of salt. How many tablespoons is that?
B It's one tablespoon.

A I need two tablespoons of butter. How many milliliters is that?
B It's 30 milliliters.

A I need four and a half pounds of flour. How many kilograms is that?
B It's 2.025 kilograms.

Conversation ❸ Language Focus B   p.127

1. shellfish   **2.** eggs

3. peanuts   **4.** milk

5. tree nuts

Wrap It Up Vocabulary Check   p.128

1. ⓑ   **2.** ⓐ   **3.** ⓑ

4. ⓑ   **5.** ⓐ

Just So You Know   p.129

1. You should go to the supermarket, buy groceries, and prepare your own meal at home.

2. an oven, a stove, a microwave, and a crockpot

3. They would find it unusual.

memo

memo